A Widow's *Love Story*

*Living Through
the First Year
and Beyond*

BY
DR. JUDITH ROLFS

Copyright © 2024 by Judith Rolfs

All rights reserved.

Published in the United States of America

Written permission shall be secured from the author to use or reproduce any part of this book, except for brief quotations and critical reviews or articles.

DEDICATION

To all those who grieve deeply

and long to find joy again.

Endorsements

"Thanks for opening your deepest & inner thoughts & 'heart language' as you pour out your passions through the pages. I am sure many grieving people will be blessed, encouraged and uplifted by your systematic narrative each month of your inner pain, sorrow & ultimate joy. Your tender, loving choice of selected words express the inexpressible. I think that every young couple considering marriage should read your book as a target and a goal of what the joining of two people should be like. May this book become a standard of marriage and dealing with the deep griefs that accompany deep love, as well as a connection point for the loneliness that comes from deep separation."

- Pastor Rich Valkanet, Living Waters Church, Grayslake, Illinois

"*A Widow's Love Story* is an inspired modern day lament. The Holy Spirit was surely with the author as she wrote."

- Ronnie Smith, Grief Ministry Director,
Queen of Peace Church, Ocala, Florida

"Dr. Judith Rolfs was brave enough to write the hard and beautiful words about her life without her beloved. I am also a widow and have spent the last fourteen years leading grief support groups through GriefShare.org. Judith's dependence on her heavenly Father makes all the difference."

- Joan Stephens, Orlando, Florida

"The tone of this book shines through so clearly. It's like you are sitting on the couch next to a new friend, and you are sharing from your heart so clearly and authentically and beautifully. I like how you've structured the book with each month of your journey for a year."

- Catherine DeVries, editor and author
of *My Time with God*, Tennessee

"Judith has allowed us to listen to the heart of lament and find Jesus waiting. She has invited us to walk a path with her that cannot be understood until you are on that path. Her invitation allows us to truly and deeply see a grieving heart, and in so doing allows us to know how to walk with those in this depth of grief, even if we have not experienced it ourselves. As a pastor, I have been impacted in inexpressible ways that will allow me to shepherd more lovingly and kindly those in this journey. Thank you, Judith, for this remarkable gift."

- Pastor Chuck Cervenka, Senior Pastor, Calvary Community Church, Williams Bay, Wisconsin

"How insightful it was to get even a glimpse of your love for your spouse, the deep heartache of losing him, and the hope you held onto for the present time and for the future. What a wonderful book to read for a married woman who seeks to treasure her husband till his last days and for a grieving widow alike."

- Jennifer Ostrander, Round Lake Beach, Illinois

Table of Contents

Introduction................................... 1

MONTH ONE
Numbing Reality, Enduring the Unendurable....3

MONTH TWO
Trusting God's Plan 13

MONTH THREE
Heart Language, Spouse's Imagined Words..... 23

MONTH FOUR
Broken Heart, God's Grace 33

MONTH FIVE
Embracing Family and Friends 45

MONTH SIX
New Purpose, Despite Pain 55

MONTH SEVEN
Adjusting, Forward and Back 67

MONTH EIGHT
Avoiding Guilt and Regrets 79

MONTH NINE
Practical Living Again 87

MONTH TEN
Gratitude For Love Treasured 97

MONTH ELEVEN
Honoring God in New Ways 109

MONTH TWELVE
Forging A New You........................ 121

EPILOGUE
Acceptance and Peace..................... 133

Introduction

Friends, you may be beginning a new transition into this strange, new life without your beloved spouse. If you were here beside me, I would give you a hug and tell you how deeply sorry I am. Please be gentle with yourself as you take this journey you never chose.

May this book, truly a lament, help you battle the relentless waves of grief.

This is also the story of a marriage that was truly a love affair, how rich and full it was! I ache to go back to the days with my husband Wayne. Now I celebrate the intimacy, the love, the laughter, and delight we had in each moment together. You, too, can treasure all that was good.

Above all, look to Jesus who truly comforts broken hearts. He'll be with you. I guarantee you'll experience His presence like never before.

Month One

Numbing Reality, Enduring the Unendurable

"Oh Jesus, heavy tears again, gasping for breath. Lord, You made us amazing together. How I long for my husband! The timing of Wayne's death wasn't my will or his, but Yours Lord. I must trust in Your plan for His life and mine, and believe in Your mercy. Moving forward in life without him seems impossible."

Every morning I awake mindful of who I am and where I am and with this comes a plunge into deep sadness. I thank Jesus for getting me through the night. Wayne's absence agonizes me and the pain never goes away. It's here for me every new day, waiting to climb into my heart afresh. How do I disassociate somehow from constant thoughts of missing my man, and do I even really want to? I wander through our house sad for what won't be here again.

But I'm not without comfort. Two weeks after Wayne's death I sense Wayne saying, "Sweetie, here's the new plan. Every day, every decision, ask God. He's always with you and He will guide you in your spirit moment by moment. He's not leaving you alone. God allows me to be with you supernaturally. This is not common sense, it's uncommon sense, which we both know is powerful. Satan wants you to despair. I don't! After 65 years together, God knew I wouldn't be happy if I had to see you sorrowful, so I'm going to be your supernatural inspiration until we're together again in heaven."

My precious husband! I thank him for loving me so well. He's the man who liked to snuggle me every day with a blanket and tuck me in. Now I awake from a nap and sob, "You'll never cover me again." I sense his heart say, "Lay down and watch. I love you."

Since Wayne entered heaven, I occasionally tell the Lord, "I don't mean to say you're not enough Jesus. I know You are, but it feels like You're not." I was used to sensing my best buddy's physical presence in the world even when he wasn't directly beside me. We did our own work, and had separate responsibilities. But every day I knew Wayne was breathing the same earthly air and we'd be together again at day's end.

I survive the first weeks by concentrating on honoring my husband's memory through Celebration of Life services. My family faithfully surrounds me as we select music and pictures. They help with every detail, yet give me final say. I'm numb, but functioning on amazingly little sleep.

So how do I adjust now? Exactly what was it about my husband that I can't live without? I can't answer that question in any rational way. I appear to live naturally with ease and a degree of comfort as I go about my day, but it's a facade. I must remind myself to standup straight, because my shoulders bend over with this heavy burden of grief that goes with me everywhere.

I tell myself to rejoice in all things for this is my new world that the Father has allowed. His Word tells me I am to give thanks in all circumstances. I post that Scripture on my refrigerator. God's plan, His will, is good. God is devoted to my good. Sometimes good is very hard.

I try to remember what it feels like to be held in Wayne's arms or have him casually toss his arm around me when we're out. I witness other couples displaying affection for one another. I am happy for them and sad for me. Sometimes for a few seconds I experience the feeling of snuggling up against Wayne.

Oh God, what is so important for me to do alone that You chose to leave me here to do? Show me please, so I may complete my mission and be done.

Emotionally, I've tried conjuring up Wayne's bad qualities that annoyed me – sometimes his stories were too long and repetitious, not that I truly minded. We were married sixty years after a five-year courtship, long enough to adjust well to one another's faults.

Learning to live without the love of my life these past weeks has surely been the hardest thing I've ever done. Second in comparison only to what it might be like trying to find joy and meaning in life without God. Even the thought is unbearable. Quite honestly, I am inwardly a human wreck. I can disguise it rather well. I put make-up on every morning, wash my clothes, vacuum the house when necessary. Numbly I make constant decisions and handle endless paperwork.

Truly, I long for life to be beautiful again. Endurable, manageable I strive for, but beauty and joy elude me. I counsel myself that my life as a woman loved by God is meant to be enjoyed. Is such a thing possible now?

The pain of loss is like a huge stone hanging around my neck and pressing on my heart. I reread the book of Ecclesiastes and agree with Solomon's viewpoint that life is often meaningless. Solomon expresses the value of finding pleasure in work, good food and avoiding over exertion.

Not by choice am I alone. I held my husband in my arms and nursed him for seven months during his final illness. Many days seemed as if it would be his last on earth. I would have gladly continued caring for him forever. Sadly, Wayne's body on earth ceased to be a worthy vessel for all he is. It became totally broken and his spirit eventually sought to be free and whole in heaven. I wanted that for Wayne too. I knew his absence would be hard, but never did I expect anything like this. I can scarcely survive without him.

I had longed for Wayne to be healed and at one point thought it was happening. How I wanted more of him and more of "us". The end came way too quickly. I still can't wrap my mind around it. We were going to survive this despite his physical limitations, do whatever it took, handle whatever the impediments as long as we still had life.

Then suddenly on top of lung and heart challenges, Wayne's back pain began. Satan must've heard me the day I said, "At least you don't have pain." We rejoiced in that. Then the pain came.

I can't get my mind around a life without him. Just can't figure it out. Was God's plan perfect? Is God the ultimate authority over the timing of life and death or doctors? I know the answer, but I've had all these thoughts, felt all these emotions.

Wayne repeatedly said during his last two weeks that he wasn't afraid to die, but he didn't want to leave me. How I didn't want him to! I couldn't bear to see his physical pain with no hope of ending it. I understood fully that his only sadness was being without me for a time. I assured him I wouldn't be long. I said to wait for me near the gate. I wanted to be brave for him because he was so sad. But I didn't want our love story, our life together, to ever end.

Wayne made it very clear that he was so ready to meet Jesus face to face. He never doubted for a second that Jesus would be awaiting his arrival. Accepting Wayne's decision to enter hospice was my last and greatest act as his help-mate.

Now part of my heart is missing. All I have is a huge hole created by his absence. Nothing seems worth doing or significant. The pain I carry every moment seems to double my body weight. Maybe others can't see my heaviness, but I feel it every second. I know that broken heart syndrome is real and I've often wondered if I have it.

The irony is that I'm a marriage and family therapist. I've led grief workshops and counseled others through loss. I know what to say and do, but nothing works for me now.

I choose not to take antidepressants, even though they're a viable option that I've often recommended for clients. I don't want to numb myself to the reality of my feelings. I seek out friends to confide in and try to find new ways to bring meaning into my life. Yet it seems like all meaning is lost forever.

I loved my life before, and I never chose, nor desired, this one as a widow. But then I catch myself in a tsunami of gratitude. I'm in awe that I have known a love like Wayne's. I feel deep compassion for women who desired to be married, but marriage wasn't God's plan for their future. I have so much to be thankful for, Lord! Help me stop my negative thoughts. I don't complain or grumble out loud, but isn't my spirit doing exactly that when I object to my life as it is now? "Forgive me, Lord, forgive me."

This feeling of powerless is very real. I want to stop feeling victimized and guard against self-pity. I remind myself that Wayne thought life could be good for me again or he would not have had the peace, coupled with sadness, when he said goodbye and journeyed to Jesus.

My constant prayer is that God will guide me through my days and I'll make choices honoring to Him. I long to be courageous and celebrate knowing my husband is in the presence of Jesus. After Wayne died, I hoped I would feel relieved knowing he was free from his debilitating pain. Instead I am blindsided by the tortuous pain of living without my beloved. I pray the day may come when I can rejoice fully without this prevailing heaviness that diminishes my delight over where he is.

I want to please my heavenly Father like Jesus did. I remind myself that eternity with Jesus is more important than this life. "Eye has not seen, nor ear heard, nor can the mind of man imagine the wonders God has prepared for those who love Him." 1 Corinthians 2:9. Lord, I truly do want to rejoice for my husband, but his absence is so hard.

Month Two

Trusting God's Plan

Two months ago my world changed. I mark this in my journal today, then take a nap and cry myself to sleep. Do I ever not cry myself to sleep? I ask God to continue to guide me while I remain earthbound. These past weeks I've learned that grief is incredibly deep and physical, as well as emotional. Just when I think I may have adjusted to this huge loss, I get blindsided by heavy sorrow again.

I still cry daily as I walk around the house, but not racking sobs. The first weeks I didn't think I would survive, yet I did only by the grace of Our Lord. I never knew the human body could hold so many tears. End-of-life paperwork is overwhelming. I know God is helping me through - I don't have the wisdom or energy to do anything without Him.

I remember Wayne's morning greetings to me each day: "This is the day the Lord has made, we will rejoice in it" and "God's given us another day together." I feel the tiniest shiver of happiness at the thought. I smile within and imagine him sitting beside me.

Now I'm a widow! How I dislike that word! I've come to realize that there are multiple aspects to this. I had an amazing love affair with my husband who truly was my companion and coworker for Christ. The loss of his personhood creates unimaginable agony. How can the world around me continue much the same? Other people's lives go on? How weird because mine has stopped completely on so many levels.

"Lord, I pray with a measure of assurance that Wayne left for a reason known to You. Now show me please what it is. Guard me from the pit of depression. May I find joy in the beauty of Your creation every day, if nothing else."

We literally walked through Wayne's dying together and I feel like a huge part of me died too. I know I did all I could at the time in the medical circumstances we walked through.

When I awake this second month without him, cannonballs press on my heart. I make myself get up and move. I can never think of anything enticing to eat for breakfast. It used to be my favorite meal.

The Lord reminds me, "Wayne was first of all Mine. He always was and always will be. He was yours only for a time. Wayne was my greatest gift to you. Now I want to reward him for being a worthy follower of Mine."

I need to reflect on that often. "Yes, Lord," I answer in my heart. "I understand that, but it's still so painful not to have Wayne with me on earth."

How many times have I reviewed our final weeks, months, days? I may be hurting myself by looking back, but I'm not ready to stop.

Perhaps everyone who loses their spouse questions if the timing and the circumstances were right. My friend, do you, like I, ever wonder if your beloved was taken too soon - why now? Why not a rescue for your loved one from this dangerous accident or terrible illness?

I ask these "why" questions over and over. I sense God's answer: "Do not deny the wisdom of My will in taking your spouse when I did. Keep celebrating his life over and over all the days I have allotted for you. I am the God of heaven and earth and I said this is his appointed time." May those words I imagine being said by God comfort you as well.

The Scripture that gives me the most relief is Isaiah 57:1. "The righteous perish, and no one takes it to heart; the devout are taken away, and no one understands that the righteous are taken away to be spared from evil. Those who walk uprightly enter into peace; they find rest as they lie in death."

The Lord reminds me in Psalm 139 I can trust that Wayne's appointed time of death was known by God even at his birth and witnessed by His loving Father. It helps now that I've envisioned the magnificent angels sent by God to transport him into his mansion of glory. In his final days, Wayne clearly knew where he was going, and the joy that awaited him. He expressed this to all his visitors.

Mercifully, I was at Wayne's bedside holding his hand the moment he entered heaven. I'd been reciting Psalm 103 to him, one of our favorites. Instantly Satan spoke, "Your husband's dead." God immediately said in my heart, "Your husband is alive, more so now than ever."

In my journal next to me at his moment of death I wrote: "Wayne doesn't let go of my hand. I want to hold his forever. For an hour our hands are joined in his death as I imagine what's he's experiencing his first sixty minutes in heaven. I am so thrilled for him. He has achieved the goal for his life. Wayne loved God with all his heart and now he's with Him. I have no doubt of that.

God reassures me, "Trust Me totally. You think I would have allowed Wayne's death if it wasn't for his greatest good and for yours also? It may be hard to accept this, but it's true and you must believe I am your faithful God and Wayne's. You, although imperfect, love Me deeply and I love you passionately. You must not long for your life to be different now for that would be to question my authority over life and death. It's not okay to want him back. You may be lonely but you are never alone. I am with you."

I cling to this with some thread of peace. Instead of denying me the presence of my beloved, God removed him to keep Wayne from a greater pain or more devastating sickness. Or even, God forbid the loss of his awareness of me which was so very strong each day of our lives together. I also recall that Wayne could no longer use his golf skills as he desired. Plus, maybe our children would've had a greater challenge of care for him and me. I use these thoughts to console myself.

Wayne vowed to never leave me, or forsake me and to love me forever. This moment now is part of my forever. God values the sanctity of the marriage union and recognizes the essence of Wayne that I will carry with me always even after his earthly death.

I sense Wayne reassuring me, "Don't worry that the Bible says we won't be married in heaven. We don't need marriage in heaven because we're not in charge of a family. But we will know each other and I'll be loving on you even better than before. "

The spiritual love affair I have with Jesus comes first and is most significant - no doubt of that. My connection with Wayne is through our memories and the presence of him that I carry within me because we are truly one forever.

I met Wayne when I was fifteen and he was twenty. I kept journals during much of our married life. I have them and all the love letters and cards my husband selected for me. I've spent these first months without him reliving these memories.

True, it hurts terribly, but it's sweet agony, savoring the days of our lives. I also spend hours poring over our pictures with gratitude. I choose to thank God for what we had, even while I continue to mourn what I've lost.

I remember again Wayne's painful times during his illness, because they help with the letting go. The nights I'd help Wayne walk to the bedroom because he didn't have the strength. My strong athlete.

Several months before he died Wayne made the decision to accept graciously being confined to a wheelchair if necessary because of lung and heart issues. If this must be our new lot in life we could accept it as long as we could be together. Then came Wayne's excruciating back pain. He could no longer even sit, nor could I touch him without horrendous pain.

I ponder pain and the mystery of death and life. "Lord, as we age You remove our health from us gently piece by piece. Our legs can't function well, walking becomes painful, our lungs can't inhale your beautiful air. Cartilage disappears and bone on bone pain begins in the spine. Slowly or suddenly You remove the abilities that make for a functioning life. We can't see or hear."

It becomes easier to say in our heart, "Enough is enough. Take me home Lord." This was true for Wayne.

How can I ever forget the plaintive sound of Wayne's voice when he looked at me the day before he expected death. He said through tears, "I'm looking forward to heaven, I just don't want to leave you."

It helped prepare me a little that Wayne's last two weeks on earth he had near death experiences. He started hearing invisible dogs barking behind him. He loved all animals, but especially dogs. Also Wayne heard voices of people around him when no one was there. He said they were speaking in other languages - the cloud of witnesses? I asked him if it was a pleasant sound and he said yes. This comforts me now.

Still, how could I peacefully let him go? At the time it seemed essential, there was no recourse for his pain, he was tortured, but Lord couldn't something else be done? No, I mustn't look back.

I recall our happy life together. In addition to being a mom and homemaker I worked outside our home first as a teacher, next a marriage and family counselor, then writing books and public speaking all of which Wayne fully supported. We even became co-authors and speakers. Few knew how much my dear husband inspired and encouraged all my activities.

I smile at the thought that Wayne didn't care that I'd never cooked when we married. He said I'd learn, he just wanted me in his universe. He was pleased to be anywhere with me.

"Oh Jesus, I remember all my diligent efforts within our home to keep it nicely decorated, clean, and orderly for him because it reflected us. None of that matters now. I'm barely aware of my surroundings."

When I look in the mirror, I can't recognize myself. I function in a numb state with silent terror in my poor body that recognizes things aren't the way they're supposed to be, and never will be again. Why should I try to restore a spirit of equanimity, when sadness continues to thrive? After several months of debilitating sorrow, I realize this is also spiritual battle. I mustn't succumb to despair.

The horrible truth is that I have never felt such disorientation before. The core of who I am is shaken - some days seemingly blown apart. I've never known this depth of loneliness a human being can feel. I know I'm never truly alone, God is present, but I confess this thought doesn't give me the emotional comfort I long for.

Heaven looks so much more attractive now that my husband resides there. The longing appears out of nowhere with increasing frequency. I reject it, God's in charge of my departure time, not me. I'm trying to adjust, really, but it often seems impossible.

"Nothing is impossible for God." Luke 1:37. I trust You, Lord, and offer sacrificially everything we've been through for Your glory. "Every good and perfect gift is from above, coming down from the Father of the heavenly lights, Who does not change like shifting shadows." James 1:17

Month Three

Heart Language, Spouse's Imagined Words

"Oh God, it's so hard to wake up every day and feel the sense of isolation caused by my husband's absence as it consumes me. I want life to be right and good again." Wayne helped me live well by his attentive listening, encouragement and insights. I truly doubt I can be as effective without him.

I have a new way to describe my plight - missing all four limbs and having only a stump left that's me. I tell my friends who still have husbands to cherish every moment, say every word of appreciation to one another, share your deepest feelings, say all the I'm sorry's you ever for one second thought you should say. You'll be so happy that you did if your beloved leaves earth and memories of these conversations become your treasure.

You have been gifted with your partner's thoughts and feelings. Treasure them. One day these memories may be all you have left. And it will be almost enough.

"Lord, it's been several months. How may I disassociate appropriately from Wayne enough to be content living without him? I am a person who doesn't like to lose a scarf and will hunt everywhere for a missing article. Now I lost a human being, the one I loved most of all! Gone from my life forever. How can this be true?"

Over and over I cry out, "Are you sure God?" No way does it feel like I can handle life without my husband. Even the mundane things are stressful. Who do I call to seal the driveway? Should I have a dead tree taken down or leave it to decay naturally? The furnace went out, Lord.

I admit that I feared Wayne's end was near. I had at least a brief forewarning. Some widows have none. But whether it's a sudden death or after a lingering illness, the death of a spouse is traumatic and fragmenting. Either way, the sorrow is incredible as the human body tries to adapt to inconceivable loss.

I'm amazed and blessed greatly by what I call our heart language, an inner conversation with Wayne that I experience in my imagination. It blesses and comforts me as I walk through this greatest challenge I've ever known.

I imagine Wayne saying "That's right sweetie. We have loved each other deeply and well. Your sadness over the loss of my physical presence is natural and will continue at times, but mustn't overwhelm you."

My first birthday without Wayne comes three months after he entered heaven. I planned a ten-day trip to Israel with my adult daughter because the first few months alone I seriously wanted to die. I needed something in the future to commit myself to doing. I traveled to Israel thirty years ago with Wayne, and felt close to Jesus and Wayne. I longed to feel this closeness again.

In Israel I imagined Wayne saying in our heart language as I cried myself to sleep, "Happy Birthday, sweetheart! You're going to love birthdays in heaven. Every day is like a birthday. I can't wait for you to see these angels."

I also sensed Wayne saying to me. "I don't have old hands any more. You're going to love my new hands sweetie." And I respond, "I can't wait to hold your hand again my beloved."

In no way does this internal, imagined conversation compare with my past physical talks with my husband. Nor have my frequent, unpredictable tears ended. But nevertheless it's comforting to imagine Wayne's words in my heart. They have brought me through some difficult moments of grief.

Perhaps this will seem like a revolutionary way to deal with grief after losing the one that you feel you cannot live without. I can best explain this heart language I experience after Wayne's death as the essence of him permeating my mind and heart.

For instance, I imagine this conversation. Wayne says, "Thank you sweetie for respecting my decision to start hospice. It was time. I saw only more suffering ahead for us both. God said enough! You were a wonderful caregiver. What a beautiful death I had alone with you as you held my hand and read Psalm 103 with our family nearby.

It was amazing. I wish you could've seen the angels who came to escort me."

Next, I hear him say through heart language, "It's all right. Please don't cry. I'm okay and you're going to be okay too. We gave death a mighty fight. And we lived well together our sixty years. Ours was a real love affair to remember!"

I respond in my heart: 'It was so hard to let you go."

My heart heard Wayne remind me, "Remember among my last words spoken to you through tears were 'I'm ready to be with Jesus, I just don't want to leave you.'"

Yes, and my response was, "I couldn't bear to watch your intense pain and diminished life. But I would have gone on nursing you forever. It was my honor and privilege. How many times did I tell you that?"

I imagine his answer, "You directed the details of my departure so well sweetie, as you always managed everything. I made the decisions and you executed. What a great team we are and still will be. As always God's will is perfect and we can accept and celebrate it. Now make the most of these remaining days you have on earth precious."

I say, "I will try for God and for you, but truly I don't know how to live without you."

He says, "It's okay sweetie. We're still united, just in a new way. We became one on the day of our marriage and God and I are with you. We won't leave you ever."

This may seem incredible, my friend, but I truly imagine Wayne speaking in my heart like this. His voice pops up when I'm not expecting it. I can imagine his words. Having an intimate awareness of what he would most likely say to me comforts me.

I can't create his actual voice or summon him. That would be wrong, but I know that this internal conversation is wholesome, holy and good.

Because of this, I don't grieve as someone who doesn't have comfort. Wayne's essence is real, although he cannot be seen, nor can you see angels. I know husbands and wives alive on earth who complete one another's sentences or have the same thought at the same time.

When you become one through marriage and have been together a number of years (sixty-five for us including our courtship) you know your spouse very well. You're aware of how he reacts to things, and what he'd say on certain occasions. This knowledge doesn't end with your spouse's death.

Why should it be surprising that I can imagine Wayne's voice speaking in my mind after our countless decades of conversations? My heart has absorbed what he thinks, my mind knows what he would be saying.

Heart language, this intimate inner dialogue, can be for any one. God gives every married couple who knew each other well the ability to imagine one another's responses. What a comforting reality! This continues a sense of closeness through memory of your beloved's words and phrases implanted in your heart. It's not a continual dialogue, just a sweet memory presence that can spring into your head when appropriate.

In no way am I suggesting you consult a medium, attend seances, or engage in any unbiblical practices to conjure up your loved one. Scriptures clearly forbid this. You may be tempted, but oppose any unbiblical efforts at attempting to contact your deceased person.

The Bible speaks against the practice of consulting wizards, demonic spirits. Deuteronomy Chapter 18:11 says: "There should not be found among you anyone that makes his son or his daughter to pass through fire or that uses divination or an observer of the times or an enchanter or a witch or a charmer, or a consulter with familiar spirits, or a wizard, or a necromancer."

And in Leviticus 19:31 "Do not turn to mediums or necromancers; do not seek them out, and so make yourselves unclean by them: I am the Lord your God." And finally Leviticus 20:6 "And the soul that turns after such as have familiar spirits, and after wizards, to go a whoring after them, I will even set my face against that soul, and will cut him off from among his people."

On the other hand, heart language is valid and shouldn't seem unusual. Our loved ones are forever present in a special way in our hearts. Intimate knowledge of them helps us easily imagine their words.

My friend, may this heart connection help make those tough days, when the pain of your husband's absence devastates you, be a little more bearable, along with the sure knowledge that one day you will be together again.

Isaiah 46:4 "Even to your old age and grey hairs I am He, I am He Who will sustain you. I have made you and I will carry you; I will sustain you and I will rescue you." I receive comfort from this and from my husband's imagined words which I absorb into my mind and heart. "Don't cry, sweetie, don't grieve as one without hope."

Month Four

Broken Heart, God's Grace

Sometimes, I check the weather and wonder what it's like in heaven this day. I firmly believe heaven is not the invention of man, but a real place. Wayne and I both understood this. I study heaven intensely now. What's it truly like?

A kingdom, a city, a marketplace is how heaven is described in various places of Scripture. Six hundred times it's mentioned, but my favorite description is in the Gospel of John, Chapter 14. Heaven is my Father's house. What a warm and wonderful feeling this creates in me.

Descriptions about the beautiful jewels adorning the glorious streets sound exciting. But I know the sight of my

Savior, my beloved husband and all my loved ones who have entered heaven before me will be way more magnificent than the setting.

Jesus also spoke about hell as a place of real torment. I rest assured, as you can, that trusting Jesus as Lord and Savior guarantees our entrance into heaven, an eternity of joy.

Despite knowing about heaven, I'm still distressed at the continual intensity of my grieving. How can it be so relentless as to create even physical pain from the depth of this emotional pain? Chronic or complicated grief is my self-diagnosis. I've never liked labels much which is interesting in my counseling profession which relies on a Diagnostic Statistical Manual. It may be that grief is always chronic on some level. I rarely experience joy in my life now.

Sometimes I admit I wonder if these days of extraordinary sadness are wasted. Is there a purpose for such extreme grief? "Oh, Lord, I don't know. But I am certain only my heart-wrenching prayers to You for help enable me to function without constant stabs of sorrow piercing my heart." The pain always returns, perhaps not as deeply as at first, at least I hope this is true.

I listen to a podcast about what creates love between two individuals. The impact on endorphins is chemical, dynamic and psychological. Scents attract people to one another and oxytocin level rises when around a loved one.

I used to joke with Wayne that every human relationship was fulfilled in our connection as husband and wife. We were whatever one another needed in the moment and complemented each other so well. We were lovers, fun-loving sister and brother. At times he was spiritual father to me, I was mother to him. Always we were undergirded by our deep love.

For sure, our union was deeply satisfying on every level – social, emotional, intellectual, spiritual and physical. God and us was all we needed but we were blessed with two sons and two daughters and seven grandchildren and five greats. We taught them our values and they absorbed them in beautiful ways by the power of the Holy Spirit. But Wayne and I were always priority to one another.

Our best times as a couple were simply being anywhere together, soaking in the essence of each other. The sights and sounds of nature were more spectacular because we saw them with two sets of eyes. Every time we walked outdoors or played golf we praised God for the delight of being in this amazing world together.

"Oh Jesus, You made us emotional beings. That's why this is so hard!"

I read in Scripture, how Jesus grieved over His people and how deeply He loved. I know emotions are good because they're God-given. Jesus encourages me to mourn with acceptance and hope for the future: "Live well these days I've given you yet on earth."

"Lord, I try, and only with Your continual help is it possible."

I know glorifying Jesus is still my purpose. I attempt to do this through my activities by focusing on blessing others. I want to model my dependence on the Lord in all things. This is hard to do when I walk around feeling like I'm bleeding invisibly and many times long to die. My body is constantly exhausted. I move about, but all my cells seem to have collapsed into a barely functioning shell. Sadness flows from my inner being.

For certain Wayne and I were deeply and permanently in love. I read about and understand that many people don't survive the first year without their mate. Cancer, heart disease, and depression are common after effects of loss. People have great susceptibility to illness after the death of a loved one. This makes perfect sense and doesn't frighten me.

Still, I am not prepared for the intensity of the physical pain I feel as a widow. I experience countless medical ailments. Sleeplessness, terrible headaches, vertigo, food poisoning because I wasn't watching the dates on my food.

Often my extreme grief makes me nauseated and eating is a challenge. I remind myself again that our adult children are not ready to lose another parent. And so I eat, if at sporadic hours. My goal is food three times a day with some protein. I rarely cook. Soup, salad, cheese and crackers are easy to prepare.

I search Scripture and read that God comforts the brokenhearted. I cry out to Him repeatedly. "Help me" is my desperate daily prayer. I don't know how to do life without Wayne. I want him and sadness suffocates me. I can't let it take me to complete darkness. I must rejoice in what we had. And I will every single day.

"Lord, only because of You can I hope for healing from this deep emotional pain. I grasp and struggle to put my cup of faith before You. Daily, I beg You to fill it. You assure me again and again that You do have a plan in all of this. Your wisdom is greater than mine and somehow You saw into the future and knew that I would be okay without my husband for a time."

I miss being queen of my man's life presiding over his kingdom – our home and family. That's a hard position to surrender.

"But I will, I can, with You, Lord."

I pray. I sigh. I know I must figure out how to do my new life alone with Jesus. Every day I try anew and fail. But I tell myself, I will find a way. I must survive somehow for the sake of our adult children.

The breath I take each new day when I awake and become consciously aware of being alive is one of life's amazing mysteries and wonders. The next breath is my reality of Wayne's missing physical absence. How can I still be here without him? But then I imagine I hear his voice, "Now sweetie, you know where I am, enjoying this day in heaven and I want you to enjoy it as well on earth."

God sustains me with droplets of hope. I repeat this phrase often. It becomes the thought I reach for to steady myself throughout the day. Jesus gives me hope that I can do this. When people ask kindly, "How are you doing?' I say I'm doing and that is good in itself. I'm functioning day by day.

The necessaries are getting done – although often I'm in a daze because the world around me is strange. The core of my reality has disappeared. The person I came home to, the one I daily wanted to please, the one who reveled with me in our everyday together will never be here again. I'm writing through tears now and must change focus.

God heals. I do believe this. I have always benefited from reading self-help books. As a new widow I define W-I-D-O-W as a Woman In Dire Oppression Withering. I search for books on grief that might help me discover a way through. I find some comfort, but no words express the raw emotional and spiritual agony that I experience.

Ours was the perfect life for us. I was a vibrant, joyful woman. Now I remind myself the joy of the Lord is my strength but I can't seem to find this joy. I want to. I long to. All I can think about is being with him where he is. I don't belong on this earth without him. I don't fit anywhere. I persist in prayer. This is an opportunity to know Jesus better. I want to use even my grief for God's glory. I ask God again to heal my sadness so that I can be who He is calling me to be at this stage of my life.

I've always prioritized accepting God's will. I ask God again to emotionally heal me of constant sadness. It's like a vine entangled around me. Lord please change my earthly perspective. I want to be fully accepting of Your will but I must not be and that makes me feel guilty. I also feel ashamed because I have so much to be grateful for. I express gratitude often and yet I still have this yearning to have had more time with my beloved husband.

"Lord I am so selfish. Forgive me please."

I give thanks for my skills and the diverse experiences God has allowed in my life. And for all the difficulties he has brought me through like several life-threatening illnesses - so much to praise Him for! Best of all the reminder that the good things in this life are a foretaste of what awaits me in the next. If I can just learn how to handle this earthly life now without my husband who was the love of my life.

The Lord enabled me to be a great wife for my husband. I pray now to be a great widow to honor my husband. Our covenant of marriage continues in a special way beyond death.

Over and over, I try to remember that Wayne is incredibly happy in heaven, and he deeply desires for me to be happy on earth. Lord help me move my perspective of pain to possibility of healing from this terrible grief. I must not allow this sadness to define me.

If I can do something each day to be a blessing somewhere, to share God's love, I know I still have a life purpose. Wherever I go, I seem to find God appointments to speak of Jesus. I have a long conversation with an employee in a small thrift shop about Jesus healing her physical pain.

I attend a funeral of Wayne's friend because I know Wayne would want me to extend sympathy to his widow. I don't want to go - it's too soon, too hard - but I recall the Scripture verse we are to bury the dead and respect the passing of people who have walked in community with us. I'm pleased that I'm able to comfort his widow.

Until I'm also a heaven dweller, many moments during the day God's strength must be mine, because I have none. I have survived these past months, not thrived, but enduring has been an achievement of some sort. Every day I start with God, and end with God. Whether it's a short chapter of Scripture or a heartfelt psalm. I can especially relate to the emotions in the psalms and they lift my thoughts.

Eventually I read through the entire book of Psalms slowly to savor them one by one and compose a few words of comfort from each. Nowhere else in the Bible is human anguish expressed so vividly. It soothes my soul to have David as a spiritual companion who laments deeply.

I embrace within each day whatever God has designed for this final chapter of my life. I live totally dependent upon Him. God continually speaks into my heart the truth that He is enough. I'm never alone, although I may feel alone.

How can I use God's gift of grace to forge a new life alone? Jesus help me! I believe You still want me to experience joyful times. Deuteronomy 16:14 "Be joyful at your festival—you, your sons and daughters, your male and female servants, and the Levites, the foreigners, the fatherless and the widows who live in your towns."

Month Five

Embracing Family and Friends

I'm grateful for the many people the Lord places in my life to comfort, encourage or even just distract me during these difficult months. Many times I haven't been sure I could go on and other times I truly didn't want to, but God never left me nor will He ever leave me alone.

God comforts the broken hearted and I beg Him to comfort me. He always meets me in my place of darkness and sends shafts of light. I am forever grateful.

Friends and family are a tremendous blessing and help me in every way they can. I deeply appreciate their love and many kindnesses. Losing Wayne created an energy-sucking loneliness in my heart. I've needed people to fill some of those huge empty gaps of time that Wayne once filled with his presence.

Some friends change but I hardly notice. I'm no longer part of a twosome so it's appropriate to avoid activities as a couple with my married friends. Many are kind and still invite me, but it's awkward, so I mostly decline. Going places with my husband or just being anywhere in his presence was among the greatest joys I've known. I keep telling my married women friends to treasure their men and savor every moment that they can be together in this world.

Several months into my grief, I'm still tempted with the sad thought that I don't want to continue living. Terrible emotional pain overtakes my body. How can I go on without him? I confide in close friends who pray for my grace to endure this agony. God knows Wayne was not just part of my life. He was part of my being, some of his life force seemed to become me. Our joy was overflowing. Best of all, we knew what we had and treasured it.

A widow friend sent an imaginary message to her deceased husband that said "I was supposed to spend the rest of my life with you, but then I realized I was blessed because you spent the rest of your life with me." Wayne and I will spend all our days in eternity together. In the meantime, I continue to attempt building a new life, but it's not a satisfying life. I don't know how, but I try.

I attribute my survival thus far to the many prayers of family and friends, and even people I barely know who heard of Wayne's death and chose to participate in my life by praying for me. At times, God's grace is almost tangible. I feel enfolded in it and energized by it. God speaks to me in words no one else can hear. My soul listens and understands.

There are no adequate ways to express how grateful I am to all those who have helped me. In fact, months later, people I had considered casual acquaintances tell me they still pray for me daily. I believe I derive strength from these prayers. Even distant nieces and nephews, now adults, pray for me. A mountain of prayers must have gone up. I'm sure I needed every single one.

Somehow, my dear reader, I am able to exist on earth without my husband and you will too. But not by yourself. Accept every prayer and act of kindness offered. This journey is not a go-it-alone endeavor. Foremost, you'll walk with Jesus and lean on Him and come to know Him more intimately than ever before.

God bathes my wounds and often uses words from the notes and prayers of precious people to do this.

I push myself forward motivated by the thought that my children should not suffer the loss of a mother when they are trying to adjust to a new life without their father. I love them so dearly. Many days I depend on this alone to give me the drive to go on.

My desire is to pass on this Christian legacy of love. My family has been so tender and kind and patient with my grieving. For their sake, I want to accept my fate and exhibit contentment with this new chapter of my life.

I make an effort to keep my appearance in the somewhat normal range when I'm out. I try to function and have normal conversations with my adult children so they will not be concerned that their mother cannot cope. I mustn't add this burden to the grief they already experience.

Sadly, many times I come home after visits with my family members and just crawl in bed sobbing. I can't begin to tell you how many tears I've shed. If God keeps all our tears in a bottle, I think I may have created a pond in heaven.

In fact, "I sob" seems to be the two words that best describe me these days. It only takes seconds and I am again in the depths of pain over my loss. "Oh Lord help" is a favorite prayer. Sadly, I'm a very needy human being who often doesn't feel alive at all. In fact, it's like I'm falling apart without Wayne who was the glue that held me together. This is not right. I know Christ should be the glue that holds me together. I regroup and make intentions to cope better.

When I cry I imagine Wayne gently reminding me to stop. "Lord, I know you don't make mistakes. Yet this feels like a mistake leaving me here on earth without my husband. You really think I can adjust to his enormous void?"

Many times during these first months I fool myself, but not on purpose. I decide I'm capable of moving past the depth of my sadness and can begin to enjoy aspects of my life again. I tell myself finally I have a handle on this grieving process. God assures me I can do this with His grace and strength. I try.

Then suddenly I'm blasted into the center of deep grief again. Be forewarned if you experience this. I've come to accept it as natural, but transitory and I make an effort to move on again.

My relationship with God is different, but ever stronger. His presence helps me cope with my feeling of dread at being humanly alone. I have favorite Scripture verses about widows. Psalm 68:5 "A father to the fatherless, a defender of widows, is God in his holy dwelling." What a relief to have a defender in this challenging world. Jeremiah 49:11 b "Your widows too can depend on me." How great a comfort is this!

Days pass this way. I'm grateful to people who still reach out with a call or text from time to time. Those who are willing to include me in an activity. My hardest times are evenings and weekends. I am blessed to have people I can call on an especially lonely night who will care and simply listen without urging me into activities for which I'm not ready.

I make friends with other widows and invite them over for short visits. We share our sorrow and determination to trust God. I welcome especially the sweet older widows who come alongside ministering to me kindly because they've also endured a horrible loss.

Many times I beg God to help me fill the day or evening when I have nothing planned. In the most amazing ways He does. I am so grateful for little unexpected calls or errands that turn out to be a real blessing.

Memories are precious. As I said, an important part of my healing journey has been walking slowly through our marital history savoring every detail of our lives together. I don't cut this short. It's a two-edged process, lamenting the life with my beloved who's gone, and delighting in the experiences we shared and the challenges that we met together. Knowing my husband and I used our gifts together to glorify our dear Lord and impact many for Him blesses me.

I know Wayne is pleased that I'm sharing my healing journey as a new widow with you dear reader. He knew Scripture well and was undoubtedly comforted that the Lord promises now to husband me and be my constant companion wherever I am. Jesus is your strength as well, my friend.

In early December, after five months, I write in my journal "Enough of this. The agony ends. Good morning my Jesus and Wayne darling. What would You like to watch me do today? Where shall I go? Thank You for being in me Lord and Wayne thank you for loving me always."

I'm desperately trying to shift to praise for what I had instead of grief over what I lost. God gave us such a beautiful life and living alone with God is going to be fine. What amazing love I've known. I commit to no more rushing or tension when I leave our home. I choose to feel blessed, strong and empowered.

After five months, on December 30, extreme grief stabs my chest and I'm not sure I can go on. Sometimes I just hurt so badly. I feel like I'm suffocating because all the air leaves my lungs. I want my husband with me where he belongs. We forged an identity of oneness. He's my beloved. I share this, dear reader, only so you'll know what a seesaw emotions can be.

Yet living with joy remains my goal. I seek to turn every memory into a moment of gratitude instead of grief.

Lord, at times, I'm not sure I can continue and often I truly don't want to, but you never leave me hopeless. Lord, You must think I still have purpose, or I wouldn't be here. Show me Your plan, please, Lord. "For I know the plans I have for you" declares the Lord, "plans to prosper you and not to harm you, plans to give you hope and a future." Jeremiah 29:11

Month Six

New Purpose, Despite Pain

My dear reader, I realize I'm writing a lament, like the Book of Lamentations in Scripture. How I wish my grief recovery was quicker and easier! I'm very slow in adjusting to living on my own. It's hard because the relationship I had with my husband was extraordinarily close.

How many times this past year have I felt the need to shut the door on the world so that I could be alone with God? I knew He alone could understand the depth of my pain.

God truly does lift my head and minister to my crushed spirit and devastated soul. He is closer than ever. I breathe in His strength and let my face be sprinkled with His holy, life-giving grace.

In my mind I still long to be united with the man who walked beside me every day. His essence is in my pores. Not only were we close, for he was not just part of my life, but my very being.

Life around me continues much the same, but I'm different forever. When I go out of my home and neighborhood for errands and church I'm devastated as I return to my empty, silent world.

I reject the recurring negative thought that nothing matters anymore. This crosses my mind often. How can I be a light in this world when my inner world is consumed in total darkness since Wayne began his heavenly life without me? I fight again this constant temptation to sadness and despair.

Perhaps you'll recover much more quickly than I am. I pray this is so, dear reader.

A big problem I discover as a new widow is what to do with free time. I once spent almost all my leisure hours in activities with my husband. We were best friends and rarely did the guy/gal friends' outings.

Much of my last year was spent caring for Wayne. I treasured this role and generally knew what each day would hold. Now all these many hours need to be filled with something. Yes, I'm a writer and a counselor but I'm too fragmented to use these skills. If you already have a job with regular hours, dear reader, this will be easier for you.

I have various thoughts. Maybe I should go live somewhere else to relieve the pain from memories in our home. But my house is lovely and close to family members. Why should I leave? Maybe I should become a recluse like Emily Dickinson. Perhaps a ministry of my words could go out to the world while I remain housebound.

Hardly a day goes by that I don't have a headache, often severe. I've been to an MD, a neurologist, acupuncturist, but still the head pain comes. I know it's from intense grief. This pain remains mental and physical.

I personally haven't taken anti-depressants yet during my lowest periods, but I highly recommend staying in contact with your doctor should this need arise. I know at times my serotonin levels have been extremely low when I couldn't stop crying for long periods. I found natural serotonin boosters helped.

Of course as a psychotherapist, I believe strongly in the value of talk therapy with a professional or trusted family members and friends who encourage you to grieve in your own way and time.

Sometimes, before falling asleep, I think of three memories about my beloved for which I'm grateful. Or I recall celebration moments with our family – grandchildren's birth or birthday parties. Not that we were necessarily side by side all the time, but in the same room and joined by the feelings we shared.

Submitting and clinging to Jesus truly works best for me. I never fully comprehended what that meant before. I always had a husband to meet my needs, now it's just me and Jesus. At first, I didn't believe He could be enough. Time has shown me He is.

I submit every worry to the Lord who has promised to husband me. I recall jokingly saying to the Lord, "This is Your role, but I'm not feeling husbanded enough during some of my moments of sorrow. Could You please step it up." And He has.

You may be the family matriarch now, as I am. I try to guard against getting exhausted or stressed by problems of other family members. The first holidays and family events without my spouse are beyond difficult, probably the second and third will be as well.

My precious adult granddaughter made a lovely memorial display for Wayne in a corner of her living room on our first Christmas without him. Father's Day caused me a setback in accepting my life without Wayne. How could such a great father no longer be here?

I look at the wooden sign on my dining table "Have Faith." God knows what's truly best, no matter how many times I have questioned His plan for me. My thoughts circle around and always come back to His sovereign rule over my life.

Venturing into new activities during this mourning time, I realize I'm in a spiritual battle. Satan preys on my feelings of inadequacy and fear. I must be on guard against his attacks. He twists my thoughts and makes depression and despair dance through my mind. I constantly cast out negative thoughts. Satan is insidious with his little nudges. I don't want to give him a foothold. Over and over, I rebuke him.

I realize even longing for the outcome of my loved one's final illness to have been different can give Satan a stronghold. I struggled for months with thinking how I might have changed things, fired doctors, demanded different treatments, even though factually I was assured repeatedly by medical personnel that I did all I could.

Only Scripture gives me real comfort. I focus on the verse Philippians 4:8 NIV "Finally, brothers and sisters, whatever is true, whatever is noble, whatever is right, whatever is pure, whatever is lovely, whatever is admirable—if anything is excellent or praiseworthy—think about such things." How I need this verse!

I'm grateful for the many previous medical rescues Wayne and I experienced during our 60 plus years of marriage – several clearly near death experiences and probably more I never knew about. I rejoice that God brought us through safely every time until Wayne's appointed time for death.

I try to find comfort or at least distraction in service to others. I sign up to help handicapped individuals ride horses. I volunteer at Awanas to help little girls learn Bible verses that hopefully will impact their lives forever. I sign up for pottery class and push myself to do creative things, to learn.

I try desperately to renew myself, changing things in our living space to reflect that our home life is different now. I rearrange the furniture in the rooms to forget the way it had been when Wayne was sick. I take away items that bring me extreme sadness and switch colors with pillows and throws. I wish this helped more.

I search Scripture for verses about the faithfulness, goodness, kindness, wisdom, and mercy of our Lord and use them for meditation. It's easy to lose sight of Jesus' love when I'm in the depths of emotional pain.

Prayerfully, slowly, I give away my beloved spouse's possessions. I must have a meaningful transfer of them to people who will value them as he did - his fishing pole, golf clubs, clothes.

I befriend other hurting widows for mutual comfort and welcome their visits. We share thoughts in an effort to help one another. Somehow, still, I want my life to bless others.

I recall how death invaded my life before. When I grieved for my mother, my father, my brother, my grandson I never felt grief like this. Losing my spouse is like severing my body into two.

On extremely lonely nights I think about Jesus leaving the fellowship of his apostle friends to have conversation alone with His Father. Or His rising early to pray before anyone else was up. One benefit of being a man or woman without a spouse is more time for intimacy with our loving Father.

I intensify my intercessory prayer and expand my daily list. I pray throughout the day at a coffee shop, on a walk or anywhere. Going out is often better than being home alone. I have a big family with lots of prayer needs. I present them to Jesus daily for intercession. I know the power of prayer is real. It helps me to know I'm doing something useful.

Wayne and I often prayed before entering a social gathering, "Lord make us a blessing to someone and may we be blessed also." Words we often sent our children off to school with were, "Be a blessing to someone else today." and "Keep the joy." I remember this now. Joy stealers pop into my life daily. I long to figure out how to make joy happen again in my life. I greatly desire to be a joy-bringer to others.

I start praying about getting a dog months after Wayne died. I can't bear the loneliness of our empty house. Every time I return after errands, sadness stabs me like sword thrusts. A little Maltese rescue dog named Miles enters my life in a miraculous way. Several friends knew I was searching for a rescue dog.

One day while attending a group of moms who pray weekly for their kids, I mention I'm seriously looking for a dog. A gal who had never been part of the group before said that morning she'd spoken to another friend who needed a home for her twelve-year old dog. Five days later, I adopted Miles. He is wounded with only one eye following a dog fight. I am wounded, too, in a different way. We're a good pair.

Miles gives me solace by his presence in my home. He prances on his tiny legs throughout my house, follows me from room to room and begs to be on the sofa next to me every time I sit.

"Thank you, Jesus. I'm blessed. Miles loves me amazingly, unconditionally just like my dear husband did."

Music therapy helps. Christian music expresses the deep passion I feel for God. Every night I fall asleep to music that plays throughout the night. When I awake in the early hours it comforts me and helps me drift back asleep. Only because I know and trust God can I go on.

When Wayne died, on the notepad next to me I recorded the triumphant time he entered heaven. I praised God at the moment. Reading these words later helps me remember the peace I felt immediately. I have lost this peace in the quicksand of loneliness. Perhaps peace can be mine again.

I pray that my spirit will lift someday. I yearn to completely throw off this darkness for a concert of praise. May it be so for you, dear reader, if you enjoyed an intimate love affair with our spouse.

The question I ask myself is, can I ever find real joy again in familiar experiences like sitting outside on a beautiful summer day on our deck? Always there's a sense of incompleteness, someone is missing. What does it matter being surrounded by lush foliage and Wayne's favorite flowers without his presence?

The tears ... will they ever end? I know there are so many horrible things going on in the world. I have a concern for others, pray and extend compassion. Yet, I always cycle back to my own deep grief.

Doing things in memory of Wayne blesses me. Sometimes it's simply an activity he would have enjoyed. Since he loved golfing, I joined a golf league because I simply want to be on golf courses where he liked to be. Silly, irrational, but important to me. Dear reader, may you find what blesses you.

I discover the rituals we enjoyed as a couple can be sad, but still meaningful as a way to honor the memory of my beloved. One of my widow friends continues the tradition of preparing steak every Saturday night which she'd done for her now deceased husband. Wayne and I enjoyed a movie together on weekend nights snuggled on the sofa eating popcorn. I do that now with my little dog and recreate in memory events we shared. Simple, but sweet moments.

Journaling my feelings gives me an outlet for the sadness that drenches me and gives me a modicum of purpose. I pray sharing these thoughts will help you, dear reader, and I urge you to journal your own.

Thank You, Lord, step by step You comfort me. My deepest love is You. "But each day the Lord pours His unfailing love upon me, and through each night I sing His songs, praying to God who gives me life." Psalm 42:8NLT

Month Seven

Adjusting, Forward and Back

The life and death of someone you deeply love imprints you forever. Some ways you can anticipate, others take you by surprise. How has your spouse's death changed you, dear reader? I like to think I'm kinder now, gentler, more patient with the frailty or incompetence of others. Definitely more introspective.

I move more purposefully. I'm humbler because I often need help. There is much I depended on my husband to do. Now I must figure it out or ask others. I'm stronger. Maybe. Certainly I must be.

I view the world differently now, truly seeing people wherever I go. My compassion has increased. Many kinds of pain exist in this world – physical illness, a child with mental illness, a betrayed spouse, children who deny their faith. They all cause grief and I hurt deeply with greater sensitivity for these people.

When my center of thought was largely my husband, I didn't pay as much attention to others around me. If he was happy, we were happy, and I was happy. I'm beginning to identify other emotions better now.

Two weeks prior to his death, Wayne actually seemed to have rounded a corner and be getting better. My prayer was that he would live into his nineties. I thought God had granted my request. To say his death came as a shock might seem strange after seven months of complications from increased lung and heart issues, but it was.

Perhaps I had withheld my total acceptance of the fact that Wayne's body was simply wearing out. Denial? Maybe. His flesh had been well used for eight plus decades. Death is natural and inevitable. I had selfishly expected and longed for more of him. Now I struggle to rejoice in God's plan. Some part of my human spirit rebels. To walk in the fullness of joy I must repent and accept.

I also contemplate my death. This is the last chapter of my life. I won't have my best buddy with me on earth when I make my journey to heaven. I'm glad I could be present for him. I wouldn't want him to have done this by himself.

A young widow can look to the future and know that perhaps God will gift her with another wonderful mate. In my situation, I expect to walk into Jesus' presence alone. I don't know if mine will be a quick or prolonged illness. I'm just aware that I will miss having Wayne at my side. Living without him is hard enough. Going through my dying process without him is incomprehensible. But God will help me.

Then my sweet reunion with my husband will be so precious. I expect to see Wayne the second I enter heaven. The thought deeply excites me. I will be with him, I will, I will. Praise Jesus!

How can the existence of another person so greatly affect your sense of significance in this world? My heart grieves for those who lose a child which has to be equally hard. Suddenly your role in life is ripped away, you're no longer a mother or a wife. The one you most valued and wanted to tenderly care for and protect is gone.

After losing a child, your spouse grieves with you, but in different ways. You pray that you can stay connected with one another and not add another loss to your life. I know how challenging the death of a child is. I saw the pain in my daughter when she lost her son, our beloved grandson. When he died, Wayne and I spoke side by side giving a eulogy at Drew's funeral and comforted each other.

Our eighteen-year-old son almost died from advanced cancer when he was eighteen. Just the thought sent me spiraling. Even the death of a sibling can have a huge impact. Truly, the death of any loved one is devastating, and unmanageable, except for God's comfort and caring support. I'm not a stranger to the pain of human loss. But it's never been like this.

People ask me about depression? Yes, I am in its throes! No need to try to put a spin on it. I admit freely that I'm in a dark place, not ashamed to admit I am very depressed, although not suicidal.

I believe God understands and loves on me. I make myself talk about my sadness. God wastes nothing, not even this. The cloud is black before it breaks. God allows my dark moments.

At this time of my life, I must conclude that I'm in the center of God's will. If being alone is where He wants me, this is where I wish to be. God has chosen for me to be a single woman serving Him until my last breath.

My emotions are unpredictable. Perhaps you experience this also my friends. Some days I long to be with other people. Other times I prefer to be totally alone and very quiet. I often make plans at the last minute so I can determine my feelings in the moment.

I'm not good at sudden decisions now and more inclined to say I'll pray about that and get back to you or I'll think about it and let you know. It takes me longer to process my thoughts and my feelings, which are often all jumbled up.

I've concluded you don't get over grief, you don't get through it, you simply feel it deeply in different ways forever. Hopefully, though, this first year is the most intense "feeling year" but I doubt that. I meet other widows who tell me it was three years for one and six for another before they felt even a little better. Yet others move forward into their changed lives quite easily. It seems to depend on the emotional bond you experienced with your spouse.

A new widow friend I meet tells me the second year is worse than the first. Inwardly I groan. How could anything possibly be harder than now?

People attempt to offer comfort with phrases like "time heals all", "you need to move forward now". These aren't helpful. "Sorry for your loss" are the kindest words someone can say. Nothing more is needed.

At seven months, I'm getting more used to doing things alone. I know God guides me and Wayne is with me speaking our heart language, especially when I'm extremely sad. He says he's proud of me when I step out. The memory of him makes me courageous. I often recall some of his parting words, "You're going to be so busy." And I replied, "I don't want to be busy. I don't know how to do life without you." Now, I try to be busy.

Silence meets me as I walk through our house in the morning, after I awake longing to hear the voice of God and Wayne. I pray "Lord, please quiet the agitation I feel instantly within me. It's an unsettled feeling that nothing can be right and beautiful without him. The world doesn't feel real anymore."

I remember the Scripture verse "God inhabits the praises of His people." Psalm 22:3 I speak praises aloud to God each morning and night. I praise God that my beloved man is fully able to hear, see, sing, run, golf, and that he is with God every moment. If he can't be with me, that's the only place I can bear for him to be.

I praise Jesus for being in charge of the entire universe. Not a sparrow falls to the ground without Him knowing and allowing it. He designed a life span for fullness of strength for each of us and He extended Wayne's life far beyond the majority of men. I celebrate this.

I praise Jesus that our children have lived into their fifties and sixties with their father on earth. How extraordinary is that!

I praise Jesus for a husband who loved and cherished me deeply and expressed it daily in such beautiful ways through touch, gifts, words, his time and devotion. He delighted in bringing me joy.

I praise God that His Holy Spirit within me will guide me minute by minute to maximize the remaining time I have on earth. Praise is my go-to default mode even when I must struggle to find reasons to praise.

Small actions help me adjust, too. They take the focus off myself, like sending a note of gratitude to someone each day. I've been blessed to have been affirmed many times throughout my life and know how encouraging words can be. It's my honor to be a giver of affirmations.

I trust Jesus to help me overcome the obstacles I face each day. My greatest one now is learning to endure the loneliness. I walk into a room where Wayne should be, and pain clutches the inside of my chest and tears stream. Where all these tears come from I can't imagine. I ask Jesus when will losing Wayne stop hurting so badly? I sense Him say I must be patient.

This isn't the life I know or want. May I be a blessing to others, even now, is my prayer. May my grieving adult children find comfort in God's presence and mine.

I have known God is good since I submitted to His Lordship in my thirties, but sometimes now I struggle to say that His wisdom is infinite. Yet I know it is. I must remind myself of this truth often.

My dear reader, no one can know the reality of the pain we widows walk through when our spouse is permanently gone. The one that we depended upon daily, whose presence brought sunshine and stability into every unpredictable day, is no longer with us.

This is not to say every remembered moment from my past was joyful. I'm human and I married another human being. Because of that, when we were tired, hungry, had low blood sugar, felt overworked, my husband may have occasionally snapped or become irritated as did I. I recall as he aged telling Wayne it had to be a miracle of God's transformation that I could gently laugh during such instances. And even tell him how adorable he looked when he was annoyed with me over something.

Of course, I don't linger on these instances. I replace them with the wonder of all the years we shared peace and pleasure together. Now, I long to learn how not to just exist, but be positive. I may never have that kind of delight again, I know this. But, eventually, somehow, I must get passion for each day, and it's never easy.

I look for tender signs in nature. I'm blessed by a lone robin that prances outside my window at a moment when I need encouragement and comfort. Clouds in the daytime sky and the sparkling stars at night are uplifting reminders of Wayne's heavenly view of the world now. And I love the white butterflies God sends to walk with me that symbolize Wayne in my mind.

"Oh Jesus, how You bless me. Only because of You can I survive."

Seven months into my life without Wayne I traveled to Florida for five weeks during the icy cold of the Wisconsin winter. We always had gone South then. I sense Wayne is proud of me for traveling alone to Florida to be with family and friends. A human airport angel clerk left her post to get me a wheelchair when I had a bout of vertigo. Another angel in the form of an airport assistant pushed my chair through the airport stopping at the deli enroute to my gate to make sure I had food on the plane. The kindness of others blesses me in an extraordinary way, now more than ever.

"Lord, this is so hard. I'm learning to survive, but I can't imagine ever thriving again."

I beg You to fill this emptiness within me and slowly You are. Circumstances change, and so can I. Psalm 61:2 "From the end of the earth will I call unto thee, when my heart is overwhelmed: lead me to the rock that is higher than I."

Month Eight

Avoiding Guilt and Regrets

I know it's important to keep Satan from manipulating my sorrow. From conversations with other widows I find having some regrets is fairly common. Lingering points of guilt can arise and I talk about them. I deeply regret the occasional times when I expressed frustration to Wayne about a household repair I'd wanted done immediately, but he delayed. How silly that seems now after his death. I ask God to forgive me for any time I wasn't fully appreciative of my husband, and I forgive myself. What a great gift forgiveness is!

One of my regrets is wishing I spent more evenings just relaxing next to my husband on the sofa and not trying constantly to research alternative medical treatments during his final months. I wish I'd accepted earlier the fact that I was losing him and simply savored our moments together. But this isn't heavy guilt. I dismiss it quickly because Wayne assured me every day what a treasure I was to him. And I imagine his voice in my inner spirit saying "Don't even go there, sweetie, everything was as it should be, as it needed to be."

Now how can I survive his absence? We'd always hoped to die together. Neither of us could imagine living alone.

Still, at times my extreme pain over Wayne's departure doesn't make sense. But my agony is so real I can't deny it. Wasn't heaven our life goal? Where is my faith? I'd said for years that I believe eternal existence in heaven is awesome. This thought isn't working fully for me, not yet at least.

Of course, I know Wayne's in heaven with Jesus – no one needs to remind me. It was his appointed time. I hear that from well-meaning friends too. I understand. I trust, but at the same time I totter. It's difficult to accept this truth because his absence hurts so badly, not just for me but also for our adult children, grandchildren even little great-grandchildren who are having to deal with the concept of death at the young ages of two, four and six. Where is G-G pops? We talk about butterflies in the garden changing forms as their lives continue. These are conversations I don't want to have.

I continue the fight to master my emotions daily as I work to convince myself that God has a master plan unknown to me. Someday, I pray it will make sense, but it surely doesn't now.

Weak and fragile, I ask God how can I get past this grief, do I want to? "Oh Jesus, I thought I was stronger and more secure in my personhood, but my inner resolve to move forward keeps evaporating."

I force myself to select a garment of praise again, because my beloved's heart is forever united with mine. What God has put together, nothing can break apart. Truly, God's plan was never to separate the spiritual union of a husband and wife. Satan wants to diminish our union. I mouth these words, I mean them, but my heart can't fully absorb them.

God wants me to flourish through my memories of Wayne. There is no need to slip into sadness or cringe when a memory surfaces, but I do. Joy, unspeakable miraculous joy, I doubt this can ever be mine again. How could I ever let him go? I remind myself over and over this is only a temporary separation. Okay I can handle that. It's just hard figuring out what I'm supposed to do every day during our time apart.

I re-read my journal from his seven month final illness when Wayne didn't eat much and wasn't eager to take his medicine. He was so done with all that. He humorously described his life to me and made me laugh hysterically. He said his days were filled with inhaling steroids, blowing on a plastic lung enhancer and walking around like a puppy on a leash with oxygen tubing in his nose.

One morning I made him a special big breakfast but he wouldn't eat a bite. I asked if he was trying to slip away from me. He didn't answer. I knew he didn't want to leave me, but his life was often nearly intolerable.

I think Wayne expected me to be stronger about this grieving process, to do better than I am. This new world I live in without my husband seems illogical. How can life go on without him? I'm consumed by a persistent pain of emptiness. When I walk around my house, the emptiness attacks me. My mind and body recoil. "Oh, God help me please I pray. Keep safe all my married friends with spouses."

Some ask if I am disturbed by seeing these other couples together. Not at all. It gives me deep joy. I don't want what they have. I want what I had and lost. And I pray, they will never have to experience the grief I am. Love at its best is a thick, warm blanket that brings joy deep into the bones.

The wider reality of our family's loss is real and difficult. Adult children, grandchildren and close friends hurt deeply also from Wayne's absence. I sympathize. I want to be sensitive to them. I bring Wayne's name into casual conversation. Despite my pain, I long to comfort others in the family.

Sometimes family and friends share their favorite memories of Wayne. I enjoy hearing their stories. If they're still hurting, I ask what they would like to say to him if he were sitting here in a chair today? At first, it may seem awkward, but my words release them to share. At social gatherings or family parties I mention how Wayne would've enjoyed the event.

I want to give others the assurance of knowing it's safe and good to remember my beloved. These people were an important part of his life and mine.

Some tell me they wish they would've visited us more during his last months or called to check on us. I assure everyone that they did the best they could at the time. Wayne would not want anyone to carry any guilt.

I wish I'd had more time alone with Wayne his last two weeks. But then I tell myself we already had our whole lives – what a gift! Plus, I was at his side constantly, although we were seldom alone at the end except to sleep. When it hurt him too much to move from the sofa to our bedroom, I'd sleep on the same sofa with him or beside him on the floor.

Jesus lived in peace and periods of true rest midst the chaos of His life. That's my desire. Growing up I missed a lot of life lessons that people naturally absorbed from living in a healthy family, which I didn't have. Wayne helped me prioritize my values and treasure family. He modeled for me how to rest during the upheavals and transitions of daily life.

Dear reader, I hear some women say that it's possible for a deceased spouse to no longer be a huge element of daily thoughts. I'm not there yet and may never be. If this happens for you, my widow(er) friends, please don't feel guilty. It doesn't mean you're loving less. Even if you should remarry, your first love can continue. Love enlarges the heart and for some men and women there's room for another. Many lose their first spouse and enter a new relationship with peace.

It helps to have someone talk with you to sort out your feelings which can be difficult to do alone. This doesn't need to be a professional counselor. One or two compassionate friends who will listen to not only your words but your heart. These people can love on you and remind you gently when you look back that you mustn't have regrets.

I've described my grief experience as similar to being in a capsule when shock rips it apart. Unless the Lord intervenes through renewed meaningful purpose or ministry it's hard to put yourself back together. The Lord can and will help in His perfect way and time. I have to believe this or I cannot face tomorrow.

My most frequent prayer is: "Lord I don't know what to do! Help me, please!" Why is this so hard? It's been eight months. Sometimes God's comfort is so obvious that He makes me smile. Other times I can't sense His presence. I've learned the silence of God is not the same as the absence of God. Feelings come and go. God's love and presence is permanent.

Oh God help me! Be my strength. "Blessed be the name of the Lord, who gives and takes away." Job 1:21. The giving is easy and receiving is easy, but the taking away - I'm not prepared for this. Oh Lord, I sob.

Month Nine

Practical Living Again

P ractical living in new ways is hard. It requires planning and decision-making, both very difficult when I'm experiencing frequent brain fog. I know healing from grief can't be rushed. Above all, I want to be on God's timetable.

Wayne and I loved God with all we had. We believed in the Biblical principle of loving others also. We prayed fervently for physical healings and saw genuine miracles. Our unity gave us strength to minister to many people and literally see lives transformed through our books, marriage conferences and the retreats we presented. Lord, I don't know if I can minister as well alone but I will try. "Help me, Jesus."

Savoring God's beauty in nature helps. "Lord, what a marvelous summer day in our gorgeous gardens and woods! Even as my tears flow softly, I can see Your handiwork all around me." I try to imagine what Wayne must be seeing. I make an effort to drive somewhere every night to watch the sunset and spend time in God's creation.

I loved being loved by Wayne. It gave me a depth of joy that nothing else on earth could. Being cherished by Wayne was my greatest privilege. How do I get over being loved like that? His leaving could have shaken my faith in God, but gratefully it didn't. My foundation is strong. I am more aware than ever of the gift life is and its brevity, and sometimes the horror of life. This world is not without daily tragedies. Why should I be immune?

Aging was seldom on my mind before. Now I am very aware of it in myself and friends I see aging before me. It's not a morbid thought, but I'm simply recognizing the natural progression of life. We all have limited time to make our mark in the world.

I'm grateful I dwell at a home in the woods and can be isolated when I wish. Nevertheless, I make myself venture out at least once every day to go to a coffee shop for an hour or two, an exercise class or on an errand. Being in the presence of other people enriches my social health, even if I'm not personally engaging with them. Going out keeps me grounded and living in a social atmosphere. I know as a marriage and family counselor that social health is as important as emotional, physical and spiritual health.

Often, I run into someone I know or a new friend and strike up a conversation. Later, I realize to my delight that I've been able to be a blessing to someone through my words. It had been a God-designed appointment. Nothing gives more satisfaction than the ability to bless someone else's life, even if it's just by acknowledging their significance through a smile or timely word.

Seriously, I never thought about myself this much before. I often engage in introspection. Who am I apart from my roles in life? What do I really like to do? Where would I like to visit? My leisure activities in the past were family-centered and based on what was enjoyable to my husband.

Now I seek to build emotional and social comfort into each day and evening. Phone calls to friends and family, an occasional movie.

"But Lord, there's always an undercurrent of sadness. Wayne and I gave each other a special energy. We thrived on one another. The truth is Lord, I don't know how to live a rich, vibrant, joyful life without Wayne. Lord, I need you to show me. This is so hard for me."

I wonder what's best? Trying to be productive in outside activities or remaining contemplative at home for long periods in God's presence? I can't decide and so I do both alternately.

All I know for sure is it's my desire to make each day of my life worthwhile as long as God leaves me on earth. I attempt to stay busy. Somehow my existence in the world should be able to make a difference. More of God and more effort serving His people becomes my go-to-choice.

With God's help, I force myself to do something that seems purposeful like write a few inspirational thoughts on Facebook, send a message to a friend. Doing these things helps me to feel like I've lived with meaning during the day. Even though inside, I feel totally dead.

Each morning I pray before I leave the house for errands or exercise. I ask to be a blessing to someone somehow. Do a kind deed, offer an unexpected gift, bring cheer to someone other than myself. Today I gifted the girl at a fast food place who doesn't normally receive tips.

I give away inspirational print books that I authored to the financial advisor who gives me advice, the woman at the blood test laboratory who took extra care when working with Wayne's dehydrated veins, to my exercise instructor. I give away all the e-books that amazon allows authors to make free each month and pray my words will bless someone.

I've always been warm and friendly, but never before have I taken time at the local coffee shop or grocery to truly study people to see who might benefit from a smile or a quick conversation. I want to be a giver of God's tender kindnesses every day with or without their awareness.

Seeking out opportunities to minister to others through prayer becomes a priority. Sometimes as I engage in spontaneous conversation with someone who expresses a desire for prayer, I do it right then.

God encourages me to keep journaling my feelings and activities during these difficult days. I urge you dear reader to do the same. It truly helps now and perhaps will in the future. I pray at some point I'll look back and see that I've made progress on this grief journey. Writing down my thoughts as I experience them helps me to understand better what I'm living through, since life on my own seems incomprehensible.

Decisions again. I am so unaccustomed to making them all alone. It's time to sell Wayne's boat. No one has used his boat in the last year. I decide to sell it and use the money to buy a head stone for our grave.

I go to a local cemetery and walk among the gravestones, snapping pictures of sizes and sayings that I like. I decide to put the date of our births on the head stone but not the date of his death. Instead, I'm going to write he's alive still! Maybe I'll write 84 years earthbound and soaring forever in heaven. A death date means Wayne's life force stopped, and I know it never has or will.

In retrospect, I treasure the lessons I learned from living with my husband. I admired his incredible patience, his ability to stop in the middle of work for play, but complete his work all the same. He was never driven to acquire possessions, he knew how transitory things are.

Wayne was a businessman, a PGA golf teacher, and the author of sports and spiritual books. The Bible was his favorite reading material. He wrote articles that illuminated passages. For seven years he sent a daily blog to friends and family which became material for his books.

Wayne taught others many valuable life principles through his daily blog and books. Our adult children, grandchildren, greats and friends were blessed to have him in their life! I often forget how wide the circle of his life was, because I only feel the enormous part he played in my life.

I struggle now to find some aspect of joy hidden in my daily life. I want to identify and remember that there are still gifts right here in my days. Smiles, calls from friends and neighbors. I want to soak in anything good and behold every instance even if it's only a few seconds of happiness.

I make plans to be with other people several times a week. It's good to focus, if only briefly, on them, but then I retreat and consider again my empty life. Contemplation leads to feeling my pain afresh but also helps me advance toward acceptance. I still can't quite wrap my brain around the possibility of living forever without him. After our decades together and countless transitions through the stages of courtship, wedding, honeymoon, babies, houses, travels, work and ministry, he should be here, right?

The final story remains to be told. The week before Wayne died, he told me "You're going to write more books and be so busy." I said there's nothing more I want to write. He was confident that I would and that I'd be fine. I've looked back upon his words with shock. How could he have thought I'd be okay when I experience the opposite of "fineness" every day?

Yet, I want to honor Wayne and God with how I use my gifts during my days remaining. That's why this book is here for you now, dear reader. Despite the heaviness of these months, I pray enough of my hope and confidence in God will shine through.

I know my lament has been heavy. Sadly, my grieving remains intense at nine months. Over and over again, I return to square one: How to somehow create a new life different from the one I loved before? How to have meaningful activity, not just pass the days, but contribute to life around me?

I check my heart during these times of overwhelming grief. I take my grieving daily to Jesus and ask Him to provide comfort through this pain. I can't say that I ever feel elated, but comforted, yes.

In the past, I faced each new day with anticipation and joy. I'm praying that will return. It hasn't yet, but I rejoice in being given the strength I need every twenty-four hours to go forward day by day. I find that God's strength is like manna. I only get enough for one day, and must seek Him again and again to live purposefully every future day. God blesses me through His unique style of tenderness.

Be alert dear reader. A pleasant happening you may consider a coincidence at the moment is very likely God ordering your steps so that you may encounter a blessing. My dear friend, blessings will be there. I know. I experience them daily also. Watch and wait.

Lord, You meet me in my place of darkness and always send shafts of light. I am forever grateful. A new beautiful, still-adventurous life seems out of reach, but maybe, just maybe with Your help, Lord. "I can do all things through Christ Who strengthens me." Philippians 4:13

Month Ten

Gratitude For Love Treasured

Perhaps, dear reader, I should pause here to tell you a little more about my romantic husband. This is after all a widow's love story.

For sure, this grieving process would be easier if I hadn't loved and been loved so very deeply. Wayne brightened my every day. He was a source of energy, my intimate partner. I missed him greatly when we were apart, and I know he did me. He was very vocal in expressing his devotion.

I cherish Wayne's letters, greeting cards and notes– sweet memories with words of love.

One hand-written birthday message says, "My love, happy, blessed and wonderful birthday. I promise my love endless cups of hot, healthy tea and numerous cozy fires to warm and caress you and infinite hugs, touches and handholding each day and spontaneous 'I love you's, you're my treasure, you are so special' sweet talk on the hour, nightly gourmet meals of your favorite veggies, hard rolls and goodies to tickle your taste buds plus weekly restaurant meals to discuss our thoughts and feelings and most important daily sharing and praying with you to our glorious God and Savior! All my love always. The best is yet to come, WTR, yours forever more." What's not to love about a man like this?

Wayne often told me he'd search for just the right holiday card for me. He'd present it and study me as I read the lovely words. Then he'd read the words aloud to me and ask me to read them again. Best of all, he'd often write me personal letters for special occasions. Looking back, I wonder if God was preparing me for his departure with this permanent collection I now have of his words.

I gaze at the large cardboard box decorated with butterflies, symbolic of his new life, where I store these treasures. I pull cards out and reread the messages often.

"There's nothing so clear on a winter night's starlight sky as my love for you. Merry Christmas Judy, my love. Another year of dreams, heartaches, success and failures with you by my side. I thank the Lord for giving me you."

Mother's Day his hand-written letter says, "Dearest love, a thousand times yes would be my answer if you would ask if my love for you has grown each year. As a bird returns to its nest, a bee to a flower, the setting sun to the West, I return to be at your side each evening and hold you in my arms to feel complete when you are near. What delightful treasures you bring me each day with your presence."

"The years fade quickly from my memory, but you, my love, become more deeply etched in my heart and thoughts. Like the pounding ocean waves, you and your love permanently changed me and I can never be the same again. You are such a part of me helping, encouraging, comforting, exciting, preserving, a true blessing from above. Thank you, Lord, for sending me Judy – my life, my love, my all. Happy Mother's Day Darling."

I read another letter from Thanksgiving. "Dearest Judith, It truly is a happy thankful day because you are a vital part of my life. You have brought meaning, love and purpose to me and I thank God for His gift of you to me. Where have the years gone? How quickly they fly and soon we will begin the autumn of our years, autumn for me the finest season. Leaves eventually lose their color and beauty, but you never will my love. I'm a lucky guy. With you at my side I know the best is always yet to come (TBIYTC)." Wayne added these initials to every card. I await that "Best" now when we are re-united in heaven.

On Valentine's Day one of his letters reads: "If Valentine's Day came every week of the year it wouldn't be often enough to tell you dear that my love grows stronger with each passing day, like God so loved, it can never pass away. I love you because you are unique, mystical, seeking, learning, continually striving to find God's will and message so you might pass it on. All this says love to me and loving is what life is all about."

Treasured words when I received them, and yet even sweeter now. Our relationship was truly a blessing beyond my wildest dreams. Who knew what an awesome husband I was getting on the day I said "I do"! I recall years earlier being in eighth grade and praying God would give me a boyfriend who would cherish me always and He did!

Wayne had a special way of gazing at me. He studied people, no one more than me, and I believe he knew me better than I knew myself. I felt awkward sometimes wondering if I measured up. He assured me I did, always. Wayne calmed me emotionally. He had an aura of self-confidence and being in control whatever the situation. In his presence, the world around me held less importance. I felt safe when he was near me. He made my blood quicken. I knew the moment he entered a room before I saw him. His hand found mine on walks, in church, when we drove in the car. Our hands fit perfectly together.

My husband was always willing to take me special places to shop or walk or dine. He waited for me patiently when I had speaking events. What a contrast to the family I grew up in which was hurry up and jump and don't bother me with your needs. Being with Wayne energized me. I was totally content just to be in His presence.

Wayne made me courageous. We did adventurous things like taking our houseboat down the Mississippi with our little kids. For seven years we owned a houseboat and lived on it summer weekends at Lake Geneva. We took our houseboat and fishing dinghy into Canada where we didn't see another human being for a week. In

Yellowstone, we added an inflatable, huge yellow raft. I truly expanded my love of travel with Wayne.

I visit the lake daily now and thank God for allowing us to live in Wisconsin, one of the most beautiful places on earth. We resided on Lake Delavan for twenty years and were a block from another large lake for twenty-five more years. These days I go and sit by the lake water alone. Instead of soothing me, the waves sadden me, but the sound is still beautiful. Wayne may be gone from my visible presence, but his essence remains.

This man I connected with mind, heart and body for over six decades had a great sense of humor, was highly compassionate, well-liked by everyone and well-loved by me. He didn't get riled up and did everything without fanfare. In his last decade, he still enjoyed spiritual reading and writing in addition to his beloved golf and fishing.

One of our favorite things to do together was explore small towns, their hiking and biking trails, but especially their libraries and bakeries and meet local people. We shared a personal interest in each person be it a Wal-Mart clerk or a McDonald's employee.

Our greatest joy was simply being together doing whatever. We wrote together, edited one another's words, presented marriage workshops together, went on mission trips and traveled to many countries. We hiked, biked, golfed, boated and cooked side by side, and delighted in family times. Wayne was my own personal counselor, teacher and coach. He liked to brag that he taught me how to swim, drive, cook, play golf and tennis. All true.

As entrepreneurs we started several businesses together. We owned and operated Silver Sands Golf Schools and children's camps, advertising and property management businesses, Lakeside Manor Bed and Breakfast, Creative World Preschool. Once we even shared a local political office together for a year as town clerk. We loved a challenge.

Wayne accomplished all the necessary chores of life without stress because he interspersed them with fun. He'd stop work to hit golf balls for an hour or watch a favorite TV show and urge me to join him. He wanted me to be with him for anything social wherever he was. He loved traveling and entertaining people with interesting stories. He enjoyed reading adventure books about surviving in

Antarctica or the jungles of Africa. He always seemed to have the perfect story or joke to fit the occasion.

Wayne was not perfect, but he was a great husband and a kind, well-respected man. His imperfections were not in the realm of sin. I read in my journal from several years ago: "Lord, I seek more of You. You alone are my deep comfort and joy. And Wayne is my delight." When I re-read these words, I'm glad that I appreciated fully throughout our lives how precious my husband was to me.

Father's Day evening 2015 before falling asleep I reread my journal entry, "Wayne says, 'I love you. I always have and I always will.'" Sweet! And I wrote "How I love this man for his faithfulness to me! Bless him Lord for all the ways he tries to please and help me." I recorded this seven years before he died.

Prior to our 65 years together, I had lived only 15 years on earth without knowing Wayne. My sophomore year of high school he entered my life. When we met he was twenty and in college. We courted five years off and on between his time in the army, his college and my schooling. The most wonderful thing about our marriage relationship was being on the same page spiritually. We'd fully surrendered our lives to Christ and His work, committing ourselves to Jesus within a few weeks of one another. We believed the gifts of the Holy Spirit are still operational in lives today and ministered freely.

As an athlete, Wayne enjoyed hitting multiple golf balls and perfecting his golf swing. I often accompanied him sitting on a chair or blanket beside him for sixty summers. I'd read, hit some balls of my own or take short walks nearby. We were so complementary and so in love.

I sense Wayne saying now in our heart language: "We have much to celebrate and be grateful for! 65 years. It's a lifetime! There you are now in our home in the woods that we loved and made so special. We had it all. I can't wait to share the music of heaven with you. Remember how well we dance together and how much we love music. The music of heaven is out of this world and yes that's a pun. I will dance with you again, my precious wife."

As I get ready for bed on my first Valentine's Day without Wayne I imagine him saying, "We had a lovely Valentine's Day didn't we darling? I got you a peach rose." I laugh. When I picked up my Walmart delivery the worker shockingly brought out my favorite color rose as a Walmart promotional gift.

Several years ago, Wayne wrote about how our love affair was made even more beautiful by God. While sorting Wayne's files a few days before Valentine's in 2023, I rediscovered the article right where God knew I would find it. I shared it on my blog. Wayne says in my heart: "I want everyone to know how special you are to me. That's why I insisted we have a 60th wedding anniversary party to celebrate you and our love."

In our heart language today I hear Wayne say, "God has placed beautiful deer in our yard for you. There are two, just like you and me. Watch them. Don't they remind you of God's strength and power? The deer are watching you just like I'm watching you from heaven. I know you love to see our garden's beauty. Watch spring come in all its glory, but oh the splendor I see in heaven. I'm so glad we never quit trying to have the best marriage possible sweetheart and we did."

These are the heart language thoughts I imagine as another month passes. New adventures may be awaiting me. If so, I need courage to step into them and strength to even want to enter each new day. The attitude toward my day lifts when I remind myself afresh that God is in charge. His love endures forever! He guides me over good paths, and across these hard ones, too.

Dear reader, your history with your spouse will be different, but I urge you to relive the fun times and milestones you enjoyed. I find much comfort in this.

"Praise Jesus." I say these two words, it's all I can do. Jesus it's You I cling to. You've shown me so much love and comfort. I am blessed. If only my tears wouldn't continue to flow so freely.

Month Eleven

Honoring God in New Ways

"Lord, my prayer is that I may honor You in this season of life. Jesus help me!" My human mind still struggles to comprehend that a living person, a beloved, vital part of my life is no longer alive. Our relationship didn't vanish with the disappearance of his human body. This is why the loss of our physical and emotional connection creates unimaginable pain.

I never really noticed that Wayne was getting much older because we stayed very active. He had skin cancer, heart issues following open heart surgery, ongoing angina pain, but he downplayed this and never complained. When Wayne was diagnosed with Covid, I knew he might be dying, but I couldn't bear the thought. Miraculously he survived. Physically drained and weakened, other complications with his heart and lungs followed. There were so many ups and downs for seven months.

He will always be there for me now. Wayne tells me this in our heart language. It'll just be different. I need to adjust to the absence of his physical presence and believe our spiritual connection is satisfactory. Of course it's not enough in my mind and heart, but it's still very precious.

I expected this new life alone would be an adjustment, but never this difficult! Most widows I meet say the same thing. Some moments I'm devastated, decimated, destroyed by sorrow. Even though I try hard to engage with life again, the sorrow prevails. It's my default mode.

I had a nice breakfast with my 18-year-old grandson this morning and I visited my granddaughter at the coffee shop where she works and then stopped at the home of my other granddaughter and great-grandchildren briefly for delightful visits. Yet, I couldn't wait to get back to our house and be alone to release my tears. I tell myself maybe this sudden sobbing will someday run its course. It hasn't yet.

I think in heaven Wayne probably keeps nudging Jesus saying: "See how sad my wife is. Don't you think you could hurry up the timetable for her arrival?"

Each morning my goal is to endure another day, to make meaningful choices to serve my precious Lord. I desire to do the works of Him who left me in this world for a time. Not to grumble about the condition of my life or the world and to pray with love, not condemnation, when I observe people making unwise choices.

Daily, I remind myself that my dear husband Wayne was anticipating his new life with excitement. He was only sad to leave because I couldn't go with him yet. He longed for heaven. I must not allow my pain without him now to define me Lord.

Enough of this, "the agony ends", I write the words in my journal. I want to totally shift to praise for what I had instead of grief over what I lost. I will always have memories of Wayne in my heart and together we created a beautiful life.

"Give me new dreams and activities, please Lord, I'm trusting you to help me turn every memory into moments of gratitude instead of grief."

God's given me an easier life now. I can choose what I do. I try any worthwhile activity that comes my way. I don't need to stay home when I'm not comfortable being home alone and need to leave the place of my deep sadness. The rooms of our home are hollow now and the walls scream in my ears, "He's not here and never will be again."

I need new resolves. But what? Inner peace is hard to find when I always have a vague sense of something being wrong in the world. I remind myself Jesus' days on earth generated calmness and a sense of purpose. He displayed beautiful inner direction. Hopefully, someday I can venture forth easily into new situations. Now I stretch myself where I'm uncomfortable and not in total control of the circumstances.

Scripture gives me impetus. A verse that often inspires me is "The joy of the Lord is my strength." Nehemiah, Chapter 8:10 and Proverbs 17:22. If I can find the joy again, strength is possible. "A merry heart does good like medicine." Yes, but how do I make my heart merry without him?

I sense the Lord saying to me when I grieve deeply "I want you to be happy. I don't want you so sad. Wayne is very content with me. He does not want you to be so sad either. Satan would like you overcome with grief and debilitated, so that you cannot absorb My brightness. I love to shine within you, around you, and through you for others."

God reminds me again that I need to trust Him. Two things I can count on are the magnitude of His love for me and His steadfastness. He will never desert me or stop loving me. Taking Wayne to himself was not for my harm. God's love for Wayne is just as strong as His love for me. That's why He rescued Wayne from the continuing pain in his failing body and brought him to wholeness in heaven.

God asks me: "Do you think I would've allowed Wayne to die if it wasn't for his greatest good and for yours also? It may be hard to accept this, but it's true. You both have loved Me so deeply and I love you passionately! You must not long for your life to be different, for that would be to question My authority over life and death. It's not okay to long to have him back."

I need to meditate on this again and remember that I may be lonely, but I am never alone. Jesus is with me and Wayne is here in spirit. I tell myself my sadness over the loss of his physical presence is natural and will continue at times, but mustn't overwhelm me.

I sense God saying, "I desire for you to move into acceptance and hope for the future. Live well through these days I've given you yet on earth. Do not deny the wisdom of my will. Keep celebrating the gift of your husband's life over and over. There's a place in My plan for widows or there wouldn't be so many. In Scripture I used them often. I will use you powerfully too."

Years ago I wrote a book called *Jesus Time, Love Notes of Wonder and Worship*. In it I share my devout, intimate soul experiences with Jesus. Yet, I know God even better now. He rescues me daily from the pit of despair. I examine His activities in lives around me and pray for others. I look gratefully at God's work guiding me thus far.

Pausing several times a day to think about God and His presence blesses me. I thought I was close to Him before. As a Christian author and counselor for many decades I relied on Him and His ways. I knew the power of applying Biblical principles to relationships. I admired, loved and respected Him, but I didn't have the depth of intimacy that I've developed since my husband left this world. I depend on Jesus more desperately than ever.

In the Bible I read the beautiful prayers of others who have known God, the Father, Son and the Holy Spirit. I create my own close communication between me and God. Yes, I listen for the heart language of my husband, but I listen also for the heart language our Lord speaks to me.

I want all the world to know that an intimate love relationship with our Creator is possible and even more precious than the love between a parent and a child or a husband and wife. I will settle for nothing less. God's love is real, warm and personal. I want Jesus to be enough with all my heart.

I believe God is always worthy of our praise even during difficult and undesirable situations. Nothing comes to us that hasn't been filtered through the mind and heart and hand of God.

One very difficult evening, I write Wayne a letter: "I have no words to tell you how much I miss you. I see the red shade in our kitchen as I gaze out the window. It's so lovely and normal, but the world cannot ever be normal without you."

"I miss you with all my being. I'm so sorry for anytime I ever made you feel that you weren't adequate or didn't meet my needs because you did always. I loved us."

"It's been almost a year since you've been gone. I'm writing this letter to tell you that I miss you more than ever. I'm sure you've watched from heaven and have seen that God has been here for me. He's planned my days so they could have some meaning, some purpose despite this cloak of sadness that goes with me everywhere."

"My dear husband, I carry the sensation of you in the pores of my skin. I feel you within every cell of my body. You will be with me forever, you will walk where I walk. In some mystical way we cannot be separated. Your body is gone but the sense of who you are is part of me forever."

"I try to carry on. The birds still come to our yard, sadly I don't feed them. I am sorry that I've neglected them. I can hardly feed myself. Sometimes I pretend you're in the car driving with me. You had a heart for everyone and were constantly praying for people even in the houses we passed. You always remembered the pastors on Saturday and Sunday. Are you praying still from heaven?"

"My dearest husband, I want you and I can't help longing for you. The family we're leaving behind us is okay because they all know God. I just want to be with you. I strive to be content, but often must pull my emotions along."

I hear beautiful songs, love songs with words like 'You are the lover I have waited for, the mate that God had me created for, night and day, you are the one.' I remember every song you sang to me. I love you, I love you, love you forever. I will miss you forever. No sun can shine brightly enough. No laughter can be as rich, no song can be as beautiful since I cannot share it with you. I must settle for a good enough life, no longer great, but good enough will do, until we can be great together again." I write through tears.

Then I recall Wayne's words "It's time for God to take me to Him, caring for me is getting way too hard for you sweetie." And I sense Wayne's reassurance to me, "I'm OK, sweetie, I really am and you're going to be OK too."

Jesus knows the depths of me. His love for me is beyond even Wayne's love for me. I want to be fully conscious of the presence of Jesus. I'm no longer alone, I'm always with Him. I imagine sitting every day talking with Jesus and pouring out my heart as I did with Wayne.

I've experienced a pain unlike any other I've ever felt. Summer arrives. To have my favorite season of the year without Wayne is excruciatingly difficult even though I have precious times with my four kids, 7 grands, and 4 great-grands. Walks, beach, camps, ice cream parlors and picnics. I treasure them all. Hiking along the lake path I see a single white butterfly flittering around the flowers and then a sea gull above Lake Geneva gliding through the clouds. I saw butterflies often before Wayne's homegoing day like a prelude to our final goodbye.

On my stroll today a bluebird flew past me, landed nearby and pranced in a private parade for me. Bluebirds make me think of happiness. I choose to see this as a personal sign of God's love.

I wait to see how God's plan for me unfolds in the months ahead. I call forth every ounce of patience and trust, as I live out these days as a woman without the man who gave meaning and joy to my days. I long for and pray to someday experience serenity and joyful acceptance. Maybe even contentment for this new chapter of life - the one I never wanted written with my name in it.

Jesus loves me just as tenderly as my husband did! Lord, Your love is all sufficient. I remember Isaiah 41:13 "For I am the Lord, your God, who takes hold of your right hand and says to you, Do not fear; I will help you." Yes, He does or I couldn't take another breath.

Month Twelve

Forging A New You

At the one-year anniversary of Wayne's entrance to heaven I see a white butterfly flitting around me on my lake path and offer praise to our Creator. I see these white butterflies often and always they make me think of him. Wayne is free, happy and whole with Jesus.

I'm amazed at the new places and fascinating people I've encountered on this journey of huge change. I've accepted the fact that God is in charge totally and I embrace what is good, true and beautiful, and treasure it. I'm inspired over and over by St. Paul's words in Philippians 4: 6,8: "Rejoice in the Lord always. I will say it again: rejoice!" and "Brothers and sisters, whatever is true, whatever is noble, whatever is right, whatever is pure, whatever is lovely, whatever is admirable—if anything is excellent or praiseworthy—think about such things." And so I choose contentment wherever the Maker of the Wind takes me.

This first year without my husband I'd often doubted I could survive, but I did. Oh the anguish I still feel at times, but I've learned I can function despite it. Sadness waits ready to shatter me and I may never have the same depth of joy again, but I've learned celebrating God for what is and mourning for what no longer exists can go hand in hand.

Grieving is challenging because my love never disappears, only changes form. I survived 365 days without him in this different form of existence that often doesn't seem like real life. I've felt numb for a year. "Lord, I loved Wayne so much. But I'm moving forward, giving it my best."

Together with God, Wayne and I created this amazing thing called a marriage, sometimes with tears, occasionally with strongly different opinions, yet always with love and respect. I valued his leadership within our home because Wayne depended upon God. He was a man of prayer. I could trust my future and our family to his wisdom. Our union was physical, emotional and spiritual all woven together.

After a year, I still can go from appearing normal to heartbroken sobs in seconds. Wayne's death often seems impossible. How can the world continue to exist without him? I never realized his absence would hurt like it does. Certain places around our home I consider sacred, like sitting out on our deck because this is where I remember Wayne last sat for days, as he died, little by little. I don't allow myself to linger on that thought.

Logically, I accept that he's gone. It is good and right. I couldn't let Wayne live in constant pain anymore. If I had to go through this emotional agony to protect Wayne from further pain, it was worth it, but horrendously difficult. As if I had a choice. I didn't, but God did. And He chose to take my beloved to a better place. Exactly what any loving papa would do for a beloved son.

This past year God has shown me that He is enough. Doing life with Him alone can still be good. He has helped me endure this suffering. Suffering works invisibly within my spirit to refine me. This powerful thought blesses me.

I determine to commemorate the year anniversary and make it a celebration of the day that Wayne entered heaven. Our family gathers for a meal, we laugh and cry together. I ask each person to share one special memory of their time with dad/grandpa and recite one Scripture verse that has comforted them this past year. My family is incredibly kind and sensitive to my sorrow even as they grieve their loss.

I celebrate my precious husband's new life. Wayne needs nothing - he's face to face with Jesus. My family members still require healing. It's been a hard year in many ways for each of us.

I find a comforting Scripture to share: Psalm 71:20-21 "Though You have made me see troubles, many and bitter, You will restore my life again; from the depths of the earth You will again bring me up. You will increase my honor and comfort me once again." I no longer have Wayne. Yet I can cling to our Lord's promises to husband me.

Truly focusing on God's incredible love for me helps. I sense His love, and absorb it like never before. "Jesus, I look at the stars and believe You would have made them just for me. The gorgeous ever-changing sky is Your daily canvas of beauty created to bless me."

I had a dream about Wayne exactly one year and one week after he entered heaven. Wayne walked into our house filled with guests, and I heard his voice seeking me out. Suddenly all the people disappeared. We were in a hallway where he drew me into his arms and kissed me. His lips were so warm and real, and his eyes twinkled like they do when he looks at me. His embrace was strong and gentle at the same time, and I was so deeply happy.

I relived my dream for days, sensing his lips on mine. Wayne was youthful again, probably the way he appears in heaven. He was so sweet and tender. How many kisses did we share over 65 years? Many memories, much love. "Well, my sweet Jesus, You now have my precious husband and it's just You and me on earth for a time."

I think about Wayne's impact upon me. I just accepted that I lived in his love and he in mine. I hear a song with the words "You were the wind beneath my sails." Yes, that's the kind of strength Wayne gave me. I look to God alone now for more of that precious energy and He supplies it in amazing ways.

Strangely the thing I miss most about my husband's physical presence is the charisma, the life energy, we created together wherever we were. I think it came in part from knowing every moment that I was his and he was mine. Belonging is a wonderful feeling. It makes you feel very safe in the world when you know that someone treasures you. I hate that I've lost that. It's a unique kind of ownership, one that doesn't cling or demand, simply a different state of being.

Of course, the banter and the laughter were great too. Oh, I loved being his wife. I regret all the moments I wasn't perfect at it. Times I wanted my own way, took too much credit for things we'd done together to feed my ego. Oh yes, I regret all that. Not that he minded. If I told Wayne I was sorry for anything I'd done wrong, he'd brush it off saying it didn't matter or he didn't notice. Then he'd move us conversationally past it with acceptance and desire for total unity always.

Wayne never stopped believing I was perfect for him. It's incredible how people can know one another's imperfections and inadequacies and simply focus on the positive. That's what a good marriage is. Ours was definitely that. Deep love is what we had, I know it came from God Who put us together. We also shared our deep love for our heavenly Father.

He was mine, all mine. Wayne often reminded me that his body was just for me and his devotion. His writings, his prayers, his wisdom he would share with the world. He said before he was married his dad told him he had to make the right choice because he only had one, and there was no going back. This is what Wayne believed and lived as he honored me in our lifelong love affair. My eyes compress with tears as I write this. What a great gift.

I still look back often, because it's the place I can find Wayne. Every memory stirs my heart and makes me feel more alive. I recall that often at dinner I'd ask him the highlight of his day and he'd say "Coming home and seeing you." And I'd respond with a smile, "And the next highlight after that?"

On my first wedding anniversary without him, I chose to go alone to our favorite restaurant at Lake Lawn Resort where we'd honeymooned. I sat at a table overlooking Lake Delavan and pretended Wayne was sitting across from me with his eyes twinkling as they often did when he gazed at me. I sensed his approval that I'd come here instead of sitting home alone as I'd originally planned. The waitress was very kind when she understood why I'd come.

Wayne and I often went to Spring Green, WI for an anniversary getaway. To commemorate this place, I treated all my adult children and grandchildren to a play at the Shakespeare Theater to celebrate their wedding anniversaries since I couldn't honor the day with my beloved. Giving to our offspring always gave Wayne and I joy. I knew he'd be pleased.

My heart hurts for you, dear reader, if you've lost your beloved. I know the depths of the crevices in the human spirit that emotional pain penetrates. I've experienced its sharp ravines. I long to encourage you. Forcing yourself to climb up is necessary to survive.

Toward the end of this first year without Wayne, I reread the journal I kept during his last weeks of life on earth. I wrote: "I may be losing my mind. Things are too painful to even think about. It's hard for me to handle conversation. I only want to sit or sleep at Wayne's bedside. I sobbed when hospice turns off his oxygen machine. How carefully I'd guarded the tubing, checking multiple times a night that it was in place in his nose. Now none of that matters."

"We loved being together. Just us, best of all! Every night in bed before falling asleep Wayne would cradle my head and say the sweetest things. 'You are my everything.' 'I can't live without you.' 'You're the flower of my forest.' Over and over he called me his treasure. 'And you are mine,' I'd reply."

When widows say the second year of living without your loved one is worse than the first, I shudder. How can that be? It's been a year and this may be true. Yet, I have confidence that having survived thus far, I believe I can continue. One thing for sure, love is a force stronger than death, it never stops.

I know that not every marital relationship is good. I met a widow the other day who said she feels guilty because she does not grieve the loss of her husband, a very harsh man. I'm happy that she can move forward freely, and I urge her to have no regrets for her emotions now.

My situation is different. I've known a great love, and I would not surrender the joy of this, despite the great pain I experience now because of it. To be sure, having loved greatly increases the enormity of one's loss. I wonder if I'm cut out for life without Wayne, but God says yes.

It surprises me when I recall all our travels and the things Wayne and I accomplished by the power of the Holy Spirit. "Lord, give me new dreams and meaningful activities please." Making life fun challenges me now. But I will figure this out with Jesus. When He walked the earth as a man, Jesus truly knew how to make every day special. He displayed His Father's love well and taught the Gospel to all who would listen and become His followers. This same commission gives my life ongoing meaning.

I know I'll always want Wayne, my heart will forever long for him, even though my soul knows I cannot see him again on earth. I'm never completely without the desire to return to my former married life. Yet, I do have an incentive to pursue new experiences. I pray for the gift of holy laughter again. I always told people I counseled that God wants you to rejoice in Him daily, live with serenity and clothe yourself with kindness and compassion for others.

My home can be a place of joy again not a house of mourning. Psalm 40:1–2 encourages me: "I waited patiently and expectedly for the Lord, and he inclined to me and heard my cry. He drew me out of a horrible pit – out of the miry clay, set my feet upon a rock, steadying my steps, and establishing my goings."

I loved our years together. Now I must re-create a different world with God's help and learn to like, at least, if not love, this new life.

Somehow, I will find contentment again in this beautiful world without my beloved. At this moment in time, I still find this hard, but God is God of the impossible, I remind myself and smile.

"Let us serve the Lord with gladness and come before His presence, with singing and, enter into His gates with thanksgiving, and move into His courts with praise. For the Lord is good, His mercy is everlasting and His truth to all generations." Psalm 100. Because I depend upon these words I can go on.

Epilogue

Acceptance and Peace

Precious reader, I want to encourage you with this knowledge that healing from grief is not a straight line journey. I've had days of great resolve to move forward, then fallen back in a pit of grief. I suggest gently accepting the emotional reality of alternating between complete acceptance, and devastation over the absence of your beloved. During these difficult times, God is present moment by moment. Be patient with yourself, as our faithful Lord is.

I share with you, dear reader, these words that God asked me, "How long will you mourn over a chapter of your life that has passed?" God says, "I have written it, and it is done, and I am writing a new chapter." God did not create me to remain in a trough of grief focused on old memories. Grace opens my eyes to the future. Grace frees me, grief imprisons me. It's hard to make good decisions with a shriveled heart.

Debilitating grief destroys and the devil wants us bleeding and powerless. God says He can't fulfill His plan for our future until we let him husband us completely. Someday God will show us in detail His plan and timing. Perhaps then you and I will laugh at all this time of mourning.

God must think change is valuable because He allows us to experience so much! We see change in seasons, but truly all of life is about change. We raise children and adjust to each new stage. In a blink they grow into adults. We reach the point where our body is strong and mature – and aging begins. Ecclesiastes tells us there is a season for everything, even the end of life.

Our entire lives we experience the winds of change. I know now the death of a beloved spouse is perhaps the hardest change.

Some days I feel like I'm awakening from a long sleep - the sleep of grief has numbed every aspect of me. Life has seemed so unreal because my husband's death created a cataclysmic change from all that I've known. Yet, there's dark grief and manageable grief. I try to focus my thoughts on supreme gratitude for our amazing past life together.

None of the multiple grief books I've read has touched the magnitude of the raw agony I experienced daily. Writing about the reality of my personal pain has helped me and I hope it provides solace for your future. Perhaps someday you will write your own story. Hopefully, reading *A Widow's Love Story* will help you be better prepared to move through this tumultuous experience with acceptance and peace.

I remind myself often that God's rules for life are intended to make lives safe and good just like the yellow lines on the highway protect us and others from harm. His plan of life and death is not oppressive, but a natural cycle to be embraced. And the way of God is always good. Pondering this helps me reach a greater acceptance of my husband's entrance into heaven.

Best of all, I know Wayne's name and mine are written in the Lamb's Book of Life. You can be confident yours is there also if Jesus Christ is your Lord and Savior.

A recent conversation with a saintly Irish priest blessed me. He suggested I meditate on the words of Mary, the mother of Jesus, when the angel Gabriel appeared to her: "Be it done unto me according to Thy will." Life without Wayne is now God's will. He has allowed it and He will empower me to live well.

Psalm 46:2 "Therefore we will not fear, though the earth be removed, and though the mountains be carried into the midst of the sea." God's unchanging, loving protective presence is forever real.

OTHER BOOKS BY WAYNE & JUDITH ROLFS:

Mystery & Suspense

The Windemere Affair
Bullet in the Night
Never Tomorrow
Directive 99
Mystery at Wycham Manor

Marriage & Family

Man in Command, 52 Ways To Be A Great Husband and Dad
Loving Every Minute, 52 Ways To Live, Laugh & Love As A Woman
Love Always, Mom, a miracle story
Triumphing Over Cancer
Parent's Treasure Box of Ideas

Children's Mystery Fantasy

Tommy Smurlee and Dunster's Camp of Mystery and Inventions
Tommy Smurlee and the Missing Statue

Mystery of the Silver Shells
Unforgettable Stories For Kids

Devotionals

Jesus Time, Love Notes of Wonder
God's Near
God Moments
Thoughts for Today, Words for Tomorrow, Volume 1, 2, 3

E-books and print books are available from Amazon and local bookstores.

Favorite Scripture: "Write the vision and make it plain, that those who run may read it." Habakkuk 2:2

Made in the USA
Monee, IL
26 August 2024